STUDENT LEARNING IN THE INFORMATION AGE

STUDENT LEARNING IN THE INFORMATION AGE

Patricia Senn Breivik

AMERICAN COUNCIL ON EDUCATION ★
ORYX PRESS ★
Series on Higher Education
1998

*The rare Arabian Oryx is believed to have inspired the myth of the unicorn. This desert
antelope became virtually extinct in the early 1960s. At that time several groups of
international conservationists arranged to have 9 animals sent to the Phoenix Zoo
to be the nucleus of a captive breeding herd. Today the Oryx population
is over 1,000, and over 500 have been returned to the Middle East.*

© 1998 by The Oryx Press
4041 North Central at Indian School Road
Phoenix, Arizona 85012-3397

Published simultaneously in Canada
Printed and Bound in the United States of America

∞ The paper used in this publication meets the minimum requirements of
American National Standard for Information Science—Permanence
of Paper for Printed Library Materials, ANSI Z39.48, 1984.

Library of Congress Cataloging-in-Publication Data

Breivik, Patricia Senn.
    Student learning in the information age / Patricia Senn Breivik.
        p. cm.—(American Council on Education/Oryx Press series on
higher education)
    Includes bibliographical references and index.
    ISBN 1-57356-000-6 (alk. paper)
    1. Library orientation for college students—United States.
    2. Information retrieval—Study and teaching (Higher)—United
States.   I. Title.   II. Series.
    Z711.2.B755   1998
    025.5'677—dc21   97-35183
                                                                           CIP

To my grandchildren, Annie and Luke

CONTENTS

PREFACE

In 1970, Alvin Toffler coined the phrase "information overload" in his book *Future Shock*.[1] Now, almost 30 years later, almost everyone not only knows what "information overload" is, but they also know what it feels like: overwhelming, frustrating, and even defeating.

Richard Saul Wurman's 1989 book *Information Anxiety* carries Toffler's concept one step further by explaining the process that leads to information overload, what he calls "information anxiety." According to Wurman, "Information anxiety is produced by the ever-widening gap between what we understand and what we think we should understand. Information anxiety is the black hole between data and knowledge. It happens when information doesn't tell us what we want or need to know."[2] Wurman also warns that information anxiety limits people to being only seekers of knowledge because no time is left over for them to be reflectors of knowledge.

This book was written for every faculty member, department chair, dean, academic vice president, and president who understands firsthand the reality of "information anxiety." This book is for those who realize that today no one in higher education can escape from information overload, either on campus or at home. Answering a few of the following sample questions quickly proves the point.

- How many journals in your field do you regularly review?
- How do you keep up with critical educational concerns and developments on issues like student retention and teaching portfolios?
- How many interesting Web sites have you discovered?

- How do you decide which to respond to first in the morning: e-mail, voice mail, telephone message slips, faxes, or regular mail? What if you only have 20 minutes before your first meeting?
- How many books have you taken time to read in the past year, and how do you keep up with world news?
- How will you select the best and most appropriate care facility for your aging parents?
- What school options are the best for your children?
- Should you buy or lease a car?

Of course dealing with this information explosion is by no means limited to campus leaders. In fact, current students will face all these same information challenges—and many more—throughout their lives because information overload will only increase in the future. By 2020, for example, the available body of information is expected to double every 73 days![3] How will these students find the information they need in this coming tidal wave of information? How will they deal with the anxiety caused by this information overload?

This book addresses all these questions and more, but it also seeks answers that can be easily implemented on most campuses. For instance, chapter 1 traces the interesting chain of events in higher education that forged the current information literacy movement and cites the key individuals and organizations that shaped it. Chapter 2 explores the importance of moving to resource-based learning (learning that makes use of the full range of available information resources) to create a more active learning environment that prepares students to become independent lifelong learners. Chapter 3 highlights general education and nonsubject-specific approaches to information literacy that have been used successfully on campuses, while chapter 4 highlights successful discipline-specific models.

Chapters 5 and 6 deal with the challenges that face campus leaders who commit to information literacy programs; these challenges range from overcoming resistance from faculty and librarians to finding needed resources. Chapter 7 provides practical steps for implementing a campus information literacy program, and the "Postscript for Early Leaders" highlights key areas that still need to be addressed. The first three appendices provide substantive background for the information literacy movement by providing the 1989 national report on information literacy (Appendix A), the list of current members of the National Forum on Information Literacy (Appendix B), and the 1994–95 national report on an information survey of campus information literacy programs (Appendix C). Appendices D and E offer two particularly interesting campus information literacy documents.

This book is a practical, easy-to-use guide for campus leaders who are working to ensure that their graduates of today and tomorrow are capable of success in this Information Age—in business, in their personal lives, and as citizens. If this goal is ever to be reached, higher education must provide students with survival tactics like those described in this book.

NOTES

1. Alvin Toffler, *Future Shock* (New York: Bantam Books, 1990), 350.
2. Richard Saul Wurman, *Information Anxiety* (New York: Doubleday, 1989), 222.
3. James B. Appleberry, "Changes in our Future: How Will We Cope?," Faculty speech presented at California State University, Long Beach, California, August 28, 1992.

ACKNOWLEDGMENTS

More than any book I have written, this one was dependent on support from others: my husband, Clyde, who sacrificed a lot; my sister, Joyce, who edited a lot; Amy Wilson, who typed a lot; and Jeanine Taylor, who researched a lot and kept the footnotes straight.

CHAPTER 1

The Move Toward a New Literacy

The dawn of the information age is behind us. But don't get too excited: it's still morning, and there's a long way to go before lunch.

—Steven M. Schneider

The history of higher education has seen many changes. Some of the most significant were driven by the expanding and ever diversifying student body higher education serves. By and large, higher education, with its liberal educational philosophy, accommodated the needs of returning GI's, women and minorities, and immigrants needing to learn English. However, higher education now faces a challenge that could shake the very foundation of traditional teaching and learning practices, and significantly alter current notions of what constitutes the core of higher education.

THE INFORMATION AGE

The seemingly abrupt dawn and speed-of-light growth of the Information Age threatens the very existence of traditional higher education! James B. Appleberry, executive director of the American Association of State Schools and Colleges, reports the following striking statistics:

> The sum total of humankind's knowledge doubled from 1750-1900. It doubled again from 1900-1950. Again from 1960-1965. It has been estimated that the sum total of humankind's knowledge has doubled at least once every 5 years since then. . . . It has been further projected that by the year 2020, knowledge will double every 73 days![1]

Editor's Note: Portions of this chapter formed the basis for Patricia Senn Breivik and Dan L. Jones, "Information Literacy: Liberal Education for the Information Age," *Liberal Education,* 79 (Winter 1993).

What impact will this mushrooming knowledge bank have on higher education? Reflect for a moment on the following potential "enhancements" to the status quo:

- the educational possibilities of high-speed computing
- instant access to electronic databases
- the seemingly unlimited potential of electronic publishing
- easy access to and communication with international networks of scholars
- the portability of laptop computers and CD-ROM databases
- the integration of computer and video technologies

Have all colleges and universities made significant attempts to adapt pre-Information Age instructional techniques to ones that will prepare students to survive in the twenty-first century? Sadly, the answer is *no*. Despite all the potential advancements, higher education has only dabbled in the applications of information technologies. Ironically, higher education today has the advantage of extraordinarily sophisticated information technologies, but too often does not choose to use them to enrich students' learning. Even worse, most American colleges and universities have never purposefully addressed the issue of how to use the new technologies to create a new learning environment that will prepare students to be the leaders of the next century.

Is higher education just marching in place? Ernest Boyer incorporated some shocking statistics in the landmark Carnegie Foundation study, *College: The Undergraduate Experience in America* (1987). In that report, Boyer stated that, "About one out of every four undergraduates spends no time in the library during a normal week, and 65 percent use the library four hours or less each week."[2]

How can students deal with the explosion of information and radically new sources of information if they hardly ever walk through the front door of a library? To Boyer, the answer was clear; he urged that "all undergraduates should be introduced to the full range of resources for learning on a campus ... they should spend at least as much time in the library—using its wide range of resources—as they spend in classes."[3] Although some libraries have experienced greater student use since the study due to computer access to the Internet, higher education seems at this time to be failing today's students. In this next century, an "educated graduate" will no longer be defined as one who has absorbed a certain body of factual information, but as one who knows how to find, evaluate, and apply needed information.

A NEW LITERACY

To address this new definition of an educated graduate, higher education must step boldly forward and acknowledge the fact that the traditional literacies accepted in the past as sufficient for supporting a liberal education—those in writing, speaking, and mathematical reasoning—are now insufficient. In fact, *information literacy* must be added to the other literacies because students must be information literate to stay up-to-date with any subject in the Information Age!

What is information literacy? In 1989, the *American Library Association Presidential Committee on Information Literacy: Final Report* defined it as

- knowing when information is needed,
- identifying the information needed to address a given problem or issue,
- finding the needed information,
- evaluating the needed information,
- organizing the needed information, and
- using the information effectively to address the problem or issue at hand.[4]

The information-literate student has mastered the abilities to locate, organize, evaluate, and communicate information. The information-literate student is thus empowered for effective decision making, for genuine freedom of choice, and for participation in a democratic society in the twenty-first century.

To produce information-literate graduates, higher education can no longer accept a teaching environment in which a significant portion of faculty view students as mere passive receivers of information. Instead, students must be coached through the ever-changing mazes of information so that they can become sophisticated users of information resources and technologies. They must be able to

- gather needed information from a variety of sources,
- test the validity of information as it remains constant and as it changes from discipline to discipline,
- place information into various contexts that will ultimately yield its pertinent meaning, and
- remain skeptical about information while discriminating between *fact* and *truth*.

THE BACKGROUND

The need for information literacy is not as new as it may seem. In 1940, the Association of American Colleges commissioned a report entitled *Teaching with Books: A Study of College Libraries*. In that report, some forward-looking educators faced the need for limiting the reserves-lecture-textbook approach.

The conventional method [of American college teaching] tends to make the student responsible to the course rather than to the subject matter of the field, to separate him from the literature of the subject, and to inculcate a deference to the authorities which have been set up, rather than to develop critical discernment and independent judgment. Modifications of the system, designed to secure a greater measure of responsibility and independence on the student's part and an adjustment of the program to the differences which exist between individuals, are being effected in many places. These newer educational devices are familiar enough and need not be detailed. They give the student more freedom, make him more responsible for his own education, and endeavor to test more adequately the progress he makes. This means that in place of specific assignments and set lectures, the student is directed to the literature of the subject, and the instructor becomes an aid in acquiring and understanding this knowledge rather than its source and final end.

The trend is thus plainly toward a greater use of books and related materials, rather than less.[5]

Regretfully, that optimistic prediction did not come to pass, and the reform reports of the 1980s failed to build upon this visionary spark. Worse yet, few of those reports called for students to assume more responsibility for their own learning, or even mentioned the issues of the Information Age, information technology, or the role of libraries in the future. In this wasteland, only two exceptions appeared.

The first, Frank Newman's 1985 book *Higher Education and the American Resurgence*, focused heavily on issues related to research institutions. Underscoring the impact of the well-documented "knowledge explosion" and the impossibility of business-as-usual in research libraries, Newman saw technology as the means of moving from ownership to access. He recommended that "A working group from the key academic, library, and governmental organizations should be formed and charged with the task of proposing the model for the next generation of scholarship information systems."[6] Unfortunately, his concerns for leadership did not address any important teaching/learning issues related to the information explosion. The second exception was Ernest Boyer's *College: The Undergraduate Experience in America* (1987), which challenged campuses to graduate "self-directed, independent learners."[7]

In March 1987, Columbia University and the University of Colorado brought together Boyer, Newman, and other academic leaders with their counterparts in the field of librarianship. This invitational symposium, held at Governor Harriman's estate on the Hudson River, concluded with a series of written outcomes and action recommendations that, as can be seen from the following excerpts, laid the foundation for current campus information literacy efforts.

Reports on undergraduate education identify the need for more active learning whereby students become self-directed independent learners who are prepared for lifelong learning. To accomplish this, students need to become information literate whereby they

- understand the process and systems for acquiring current and retrospective information, e.g., systems and services for information identification and delivery;
- are able to evaluate the effectiveness and reliability of various information channels and sources, including libraries, for various kinds of needs;
- master certain basic skills in acquiring and storing their own information, e.g., database skills, spreadsheet skills, word and information processing skills, books, journals, and report literature;
- are articulate and responsible citizens in considering current and future public policy issues relating to information, e.g., copyright, privacy, privatization of government information, and those issues yet to emerge.

To make possible the above, information gathering and evaluation skills need to be mastered at the undergraduate level, and learning opportunities should be integrated within the existing departments, analogous to "writing across the curriculum," rather than as stand-alone bibliographic instruction programs. Administrators, faculty and librarians should be engaged in creative new partnerships which transmit to students the value and reward of research in their lives as students and beyond. Information literacy should be a demonstrable outcome of undergraduate education.[8]

ALA Presidential Committee on Information Literacy

One of the conference attendees, Margaret Chisholm from the University of Washington, was the incoming president of the American Library Association (ALA). She decided that the discussion was too important to stop with the conference. As a result, she established the ALA Presidential Committee on Information Literacy, which was made up of seven national leaders from education and six from librarianship. The committee's final report (reprinted in full in Appendix A) was issued at a press conference in Washington, D.C., in January 1989; the report is the clearest statement ever made about the importance of information literacy.

No other change in American society has offered greater challenges than the emergence of the Information Age. Information is expanding at an unprecedented rate, and enormously rapid strides are being made in the technology for storing, organizing, and accessing the ever growing tidal wave of information. The combined effect of these factors is an increasingly fragmented information base—large components of which are only available to people with money and/or acceptable institutional affiliations.

Yet in an information society all people should have the right to information that can enhance their lives. Out of the super-abundance of available information, people need to be able to obtain specific information to meet a wide range of personal and business needs. These needs are largely driven either by the desire for personal growth and advancement or by the rapidly changing social, political, and economic environments of American society. What is true today is often outdated tomorrow. A good job today may be obsolete next year. To promote economic independence and quality of existence, there is a lifelong need for being informed and up-to-date.

How our country deals with the realities of the Information Age will have enormous impact on our democratic way of life and on our nation's ability to compete internationally. Within America's information society, there also exists the potential of addressing many long-standing social and economic inequities. To reap such benefits, people—as individuals and as a nation—must be information literate. To be information literate, a person must be able to recognize when information is needed and have the ability to locate, evaluate, and use effectively the needed information. Producing such a citizenry will require that educators at both the school and college levels appreciate and integrate the concept of information literacy into their learning programs and that they play a leadership role in equipping individuals and institutions to take advantage of the opportunities inherent within the information society.[9]

National Forum on Information Literacy

The report of the ALA Presidential Committee on Information Literacy resulted in the establishment of the National Forum on Information Literacy, a broadly based group of over 65 national organizations committed to the concept of information literacy as a means of individual empowerment. (See Appendix B for a list of the Forum's members.) Meeting three times a year in Washington, D.C., the Forum members share progress and network resources, undertake selected projects, and maintain a listserv (infolit@ala1.ala.org).

HIGHER EDUCATION'S RESPONSE IN THE U.S.

A constantly growing number of educators and institutions are realizing the essential nature of information literacy for successful education in the next century. Sometimes efforts at improving information literacy are scattered; sometimes such efforts are part of an across-the-curriculum planning initiative. But, as the following examples show, all are moving beyond the concept of traditional library/bibliographic instruction to integrating information resources and technology into the curriculum.

Leadership from Regional Accrediting Agencies

The Commission on Higher Education (CHE) of the Middle States Association of Colleges and Schools was an early leader among the groups and institutions seriously addressing the need for information literacy. In 1992, Howard Simmons, the former executive director of the Middle States Association, explained his agency's commitment to information literacy.

> The Association, as part of its planning process, concluded that one of its initiatives for assisting member institutions in improving undergraduate education should be a stronger emphasis on assessing student and faculty utilization of library and other learning resources. . . .
>
> As educators, most of us today have become increasingly aware that we and our students need to acquire more sophisticated information skills to access and use information in a variety of formats to address our education and life objectives.[10]

CHE launched its information literacy efforts by publishing a list of specific curriculum-related questions in its 1990 "Framework for Outcomes Assessment."[11] In 1996, in its *Framework* statements, CHE strongly articulated the need for information literacy as a critical ingredient in a student's general education.

> The goal of general education is to develop the broad abilities, intellectual and other skills, ideas, and values that shape a student's capacity to address problems across varied academic fields, including the arts and literature, history, the social and natural sciences, and mathematics.
>
> Among the important abilities underlying the transfer of knowledge are, for example: the ability to think critically; the ability to develop problem solving strategies; effective writing and oral communication; technological competence, especially with library and other information management resources; familiarity with mathematics and quantitative analysis; and a range of attitudes and dispositions associated with human values and responsible judgment.
>
> The analysis of student achievement with respect to general education utilizes different measurement objectives for assessing competencies in four broad areas: cognitive abilities (critical thinking, problem solving), content literacy (knowledge of social institutions, science and technology), competence in information management skills and communication, and value awareness (multicultural understanding, moral and ethical judgment).
>
> Information literacy incorporates all four competency areas and transcends specific disciplines and professional careers. It has been defined as a subset of critical thinking skills which consists of individuals' abilities to know when they have an information need and to access, evaluate (determine usefulness of, summarize, synthesize, and draw conclusions from), and effectively use information for both content literacy in the curriculum and lifelong learning.[12]

Both Simmons, and, more recently, Oswald Ratteray have always focused their information literacy leadership at CHE on the practical; intellectual leadership belongs to Ralph A. Wolff, who moved from deputy to executive director of the Western Association of Schools and Colleges in 1995. Wolff uses a quantum physics model to describe a new way of conceptualizing the relationship that should exist between academic libraries and their campuses and which is a necessary step toward providing the collaborative base required for strong information literacy programs.

> Quantum physics presents an entirely new organizing principle of reality that is only beginning to find its way into science, organizational development, and society at large. Quantum physics came about from the study of subatomic particles—in our constant quest to know more and more about less and less—the parts that make up the atom. These parts include electrons, protons, and neutrons, and this study led to ever smaller sub-sub-atomic parts being identified. To their surprise, scientists learned that these particles can display different properties. . . . First, something may be both one thing and another thing at the same time (a particle and a wave) but what it is depends on the context in which it is functioning or on how it is being viewed. This leads to a second point: the relationships between parts is as important as the parts themselves. In quantum physics, particles do not exist as independent "things" but come into being and are observed only in relationship to something else. Third, the act of observing or measuring something effects it. . . .
>
> What does the quantum physics model mean for higher education and libraries? First, the library needs to be seen both as an independent entity and as a major contributor to the learning process. It is not an either-or proposition. In the quantum physics model, the context for observation is critical; so too is defining the mission of the library and its role in the teaching and learning processes of the institution. The organizing principle used can define not only indicators of quality but the mission and attributes of organization and functioning for the library (and the institution as a whole). The next . . . stage of development for the library is to serve as a full partner in transforming the act of learning. This is an emerging role and an increasingly critical one. Elements of this new role are already in place at many institutions with changes taking place in the library, the wiring of the campus, the merging of computing and information resources, and the increased technical expertise of library staff. As libraries develop learning outcomes and then apply quality indicators based on their contribution to the learning process, the new role will become better defined and understood. Partnerships between librarians and faculty can accelerate the achievement of the new role. The main point is that the library needs to be taken out of its confining role as a support service and seen as a central element in any institution's response to the learner of the future.[13]

Washington State Community Colleges

Besides early leadership from some regional accrediting agencies, the community and technical colleges in the state of Washington undertook a significant statewide effort to make information literacy a vital part of all educational undertakings. Heralded as "Information Competency," this successful endeavor began with a 1993 position paper developed by the community and technical college library directors and entitled "Information Competency: An Initiative for Integrated Learning."[14] The paper was subsequently endorsed by the Instruction Commission, which is made up of the instructional deans of the 32 community and technical colleges in the state. This unanimous approval affirmed the concept and encouraged the librarians to implement the strategies outlined in the paper. The Instruction Commission further suggested that

> each institution develop an active library instruction planning committee to establish library goals and objectives reflecting accreditation standards, the needs and cultures of local campuses, and the changes that are occurring in the areas of information technology, the teaching/learning process, and the delivery of instruction.[15]

This direction provided both an impetus and a framework for discussion on the individual campuses regarding curricular integration. In a 1995 survey, 26 of the 32 colleges indicated progress toward "Information Competency" as a direct result of the position paper. Implementation ranged from increased course-integrated instruction to entire core courses. Some schools even instituted specific information requirements as a graduation requirement or a college goal.

California State University and Community College Systems

The California State University System (CSU) is also moving aggressively to meet the challenge of information literacy. Its efforts began in response to the question of whether the system was preparing its students "to navigate successfully through the profusion of print and electronic media."[16] Planners realized that the skills students needed to get them through this electronic media maze had applications that reached far beyond their years on campus. In a recent speech, Lorie Roth, CSU director of academic services and professional development, summarized the direction of California's visionary efforts.

> The ultimate aim of the CSU's task force on information competence is to make sure that every graduate of the California State University knows how to find information, how to evaluate it, and how to use it effectively—and can demonstrate those skills in some kind of a performance-based test.

How are we going to make this happen? It will, of course, take changing the entire culture of the CSU—which is kind of like asking an aircraft carrier to change course in mid-ocean. . . .

There are, however, three specific routes that we are pursuing. First, we want to increase the collaboration between librarians and faculty, to get them to work together in the best interests of the student. Second, we want to encourage "information competence" across the curriculum, much like the movement called "writing across the curriculum." Proponents of Writing Across the Curriculum suggested that writing was not something that should be taught only once in a student's career—usually in freshman English—and then never referred to again. Instead some form of writing should be required in many courses in many disciplines ranging from the freshman to the senior year. Likewise, we don't think that library instruction should be just one component of a freshman English or a college orientation course. We don't think that computer literacy should be restricted to just a single course. We think that these skills and the other skills of information competence should be taught and reinforced in nearly every course that a college student takes.

Finally, we are urging the campuses to reconsider their general education requirements. For a long time, we have all agreed that college students should take some English, some math, some history—and this is all codified in Title 5 of the Education Code. Now we think that it's time that students should also be required to have some information competence—which is a subject that cuts across all disciplines, from English to computer science to philosophy to film.[17]

During the 1990s, serious attention has also been given to "information competency" within the California Community College (CCC) system. Most recently the CCC Board of Governors Curriculum Services and Instructional Resources Division set competitive grant funding priorities that included information competencies as one of three areas earmarked for funding requests. The application guidelines for information competency projects stated the following:

Develop an "Information Competency Plan" as a prerequisite for the completion of a community college certificate and/or the receipt of the associate degree. This project will review the recommendations from each of the state's education segments, and make recommendations for implementation, evaluation, and training.

"Information Competency" is defined as a subset of critical thinking skills which include the ability of individuals to recognize the need for information and find, evaluate, incorporate, use, create, and communicate that information from a variety of sources and contexts.

This is a two-year project. Initial funding will be for a task force to work with a consultant in this area. This task force will work within a timeline not to exceed nine months, including field consultations.

The second year funding will provide technical assistance to the colleges in the implementation of the plan. The third year will be to evaluate and present the Board a comprehensive report on the project's success (this year will involve no funding).[18]

This effort is an outgrowth of a March 13, 1996 CCC document, *Information Competency in the California Community Colleges: A Status Report.*[19]

BENCHMARKING U.S. EFFORTS

The foregoing examples of endorsement and incorporation of information literacy by associations and institutions in the United States are just a few of the many that could be cited. However, in spite of these examples and the growing body of literature about information literacy that had arisen since the 1989 publication of the final report of the ALA Presidential Committee on Information Literacy, little effort was made to measure the extent to which information literacy had actually been assimilated into the curriculum of post-secondary institutions. Then, in 1994-95, a national survey on this question was conducted throughout the 3,236 accredited U.S. colleges and universities within the six regional accrediting agencies. The survey was an outgrowth of a meeting of the National Forum on Information Literacy and involved a cooperative effort among the Association of College & Research Libraries (ACRL), the Commission on Higher Education (CHE) of the Middle States Association of Colleges and Schools, and the Western Accrediting Commission for Senior Colleges and Universities (WASC). The survey also had the endorsement of the American Association of Higher Education. (See Appendix C for specific information about this survey.)

The survey provided an overall snapshot of an academic community struggling to respond to the Information Age. The survey concluded that information literacy is being pursued in varying degrees by about a quarter of the 834 institutions that responded. The survey was also responsible for fueling efforts by proponents of information literacy and for encouraging other accrediting agencies to become involved in similar efforts. For example, after receiving the results of the survey, the Commission on Higher Education (CHE) of the Middle States Association of Colleges and Schools scheduled two symposia. The organizers invited teams of educators from campuses that were judged to have most successfully assimilated information literacy into their curriculums. The organizers also invited their counterparts from campuses that held out the most promise for embracing information literacy. A summary of the two symposia was published by CHE in 1995.[20] The results of those symposia provide the basis for the discussions in Chapters 5 and 6 of this book.

"A Vision for Information Literacy in Higher Education" became the topic for the first pre-conference ever offered by the New England Association of

Schools and Colleges. Held on December 5, 1996, the conference featured Dr. Thomas Abbott, dean of learning resources and university development at the University of Maine; Ann Schaffer, associate director of the Science Library and reference services at Brandeis University in Massachusetts; and M. Beverly Swan, provost and vice president of the University of Rhode Island. All these presenters explained how their campuses are developing curricula to produce information-literate students.

The North Central Accrediting Agency, which scheduled a series of programs for its 1997 annual conference, included four sessions on the following topics:

- Assessing Libraries in Support of Campus Missions
- Information Literacy: General Education for the 21st Century
- Off Campus Courses and Library Support
- Assessing the Library: What Data Institutions Need

Considering the activities that have already been undertaken and are currently in development by the various accrediting agencies, it is clear that no one blueprint is right for all efforts at all institutions. The important thing is that these agencies are asking the right questions. Although the answers will vary based on the missions of the individual campuses, the questions frequently cause busy campus leaders to take a second look at the expectations they have for their library resources and personnel and, in particular, to re-examine the potential teaching/learning contributions they can make toward preparing students for academic success and lifelong learning.

HIGHER EDUCATION'S RESPONSE ABROAD

A recent article by Hannelore B. Radar[21] reviews many of the current international efforts related to information literacy and better use of library resources and services in the teaching/learning process. Following are some notable examples of these efforts.

Australia

In 1993, the Australian Higher Education Council commissioned a report "to identify and describe the characteristics of undergraduate education which enable and encourage graduates to participate in formal and informal learning throughout their lives."[22] The report, entitled *Developing Lifelong Learners Through Undergraduate Education* (1994), cited information literacy as one of the essential considerations for "Putting Lifelong Learning at the Heart of Undergraduate Programs." One of the report's many recommendations was that "the processes for resourcing libraries take account of the vital role of the libraries and of information literacy generally in the development of lifelong learners."[23]

The report documents the current status of both thinking and practice in regard to information literacy's role on Australian college campuses. The following excerpts from the report clearly spell out the importance of information literacy in preparing students for lifelong learning.

> Because of the rapid rate of growth in most professional areas, a graduate cannot be considered to be, even embryonically, a "well-rounded person," unless he or she possesses a degree of "information literacy." . . .
>
> These days, when much knowledge has at best a shelf-life and 'use-by' date of less than five years (in some cases less than a year), it is no longer sufficient for graduates, or indeed any other member of the community, to be able simply to make use of library reference collections, manual catalogues and the odd bibliography. . . .
>
> In the information age, mastery of all manner of electronic databases, indexes and networks is essential just to keep in touch with current developments in the field and to be familiar with information retrieval systems which enable the new graduate to function both as a competent professional, and as a member of the community. It is important, therefore, that graduates leave university equipped with the skills and strategies to locate, access, retrieve, evaluate, manage and make use of information in a variety of fields, rather than with a finite body of knowledge that will soon be outdated and irrelevant.[24]

Australia has aggressively pursued information literacy as a foundation for all learning. As this book was being written, plans were underway for Australia's third national conference on information literacy to be held in December 1997. The conference theme is "Information Literacy: The Professional Issue," and speakers will address the following topics:

- What skills and knowledge are required for people to be considered lifelong learners in the twenty-first century?
- Where does lifelong learning fit into accreditation processes and initial training and continuing education programs?
- What issues are raised by the notion of lifelong learning for professional associations and unions in on-the-job and off-the-job training?[25]

South Africa

Major efforts are also underway in South Africa, where Shirley Behrens, of the University of South Africa in Pretoria, has written one of the most definitive histories of information literacy efforts worldwide.[26] Of particular importance to higher education is the $1 million grant from the South African *Readers' Digest* to leaders at the five universities in the Cape Town region to foster information literacy on their campuses. The grant includes the development of pilot products that all five universities can use.

University of Cape Town Professor Wieland Gevers, who serves as vice-rector-in-liaison to the Cape Library Cooperative Project and to INFOLIT, its information literacy project, explained in the foreword of the first annual report of the INFOLIT project why the five participating Cape Town institutions have made such a commitment to developing information literacy programs.

> Information literacy is one of the key intellectual skills attainments required by the modern world, and its importance increases by the day. It cannot replace the need for language, communication and numerical skills; it cannot compensate for the lack of the ability to think conceptually and to analyze and solve problems; it is not an end in itself. But it complements, extends and polishes these other basic skills and, ultimately, it is an absolute requirement for success, even for basic functioning in virtually all areas of work and in all careers.
>
> One of the most intriguing aspects of this effort is its emphasis on "cross-institutional and trans-disciplinary collaboration" in keeping with "the vision to build a learning community in the region."[27]

China

Countries that are unconcerned with the effective use of information resources must pay a high price. A 1990 article on libraries and their use in China, for example, cited a survey that indicated that "83% of current users felt is was difficult to obtain key information." To illustrate the cost of such difficulty, the same survey stated that "forty percent of the research projects in modern physics in China are replicating projects already completed by others abroad." Nevertheless, China is taking strong steps to address these weaknesses. With the Ministry of Education requiring college and university libraries to develop courses of library user education, more than half of the campuses had such courses in place by 1990.[28]

American international competitiveness will increasingly depend upon this country's success in graduating information-literate students who are able to gather, analyze, and use information creatively and effectively. Reinforcing this idea, James B. Appleberry issued the following challenge to California faculty members in August 1992.

> If we are to remain the intellectual leader of the world, we must rethink the structure of information in each of our disciplines. We must understand that information in most of our disciplines is not linear, and that the teaching we do must prepare a student who will randomly access information across a broad array of disciplines.[29]

TWO VISIONS

Before colleges and universities can be expected to aggressively pursue information literacy, they will need a clear vision of what information-literate college students "look" like and how an Information Age campus would differ from their current campuses. With the following definitions and examples, perhaps those visions will come one step closer to reality.

Information-Literate Students

Figure 1-1, developed by Griffith University in Queensland, Australia, adds some substantive outlines to the vision by giving an overall definition of an information-literate person as "one who engages in independent, self-directed learning."[30]

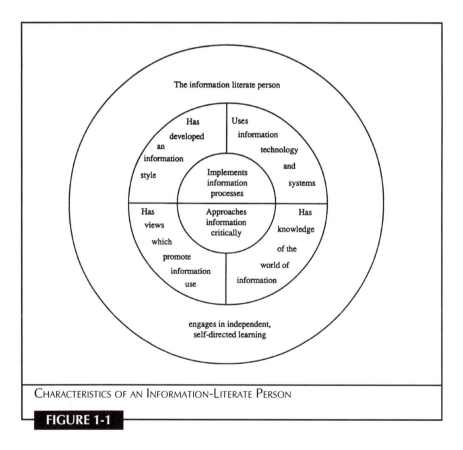

CHARACTERISTICS OF AN INFORMATION-LITERATE PERSON

FIGURE 1-1

Although such a visual is helpful, the most succinct yet vivid definition of an information-literate student written to date is stated in *Standards for Student Learning, Draft #5*, which was developed by the American Association of School Librarians and the Association for Educational Communications and Technology, and was in the final stages of adoption as this book went to press. The following definition is the vision—in words—of what information-literate students are and what they can do.[31]

Standards for Student Learning, Draft #5

Category I: Information Literacy
The student who is information literate:

Standard 1: Accesses information efficiently and effectively, as described by the following indicators:

1. recognizes the need for information;
2. recognizes that accurate and complete information is the basis for intelligent decision making;
3. formulates questions based on information needs;
4. identifies a variety of potential sources of information;
5. develops and uses successful strategies for locating information.

Standard 2: Evaluates information critically and competently, as described by the following indicators:

1. determines accuracy, relevance, and comprehensiveness;
2. distinguishes among facts, point of view, and opinion;
3. identifies inaccurate and misleading information;
4. selects information appropriate to the problem or question at hand.

Standard 3: Uses information effectively and creatively, as described by the following indicators:

1. organizes information for practical application;
2. integrates new information into one's own knowledge;
3. applies information in critical thinking and problem solving;
4. produces and communicates information and ideas in appropriate formats.

Category II: Independent Learning
The student who is an independent learner is information literate and:

Standard 4: Pursues information related to personal interests, as described by the following indicators:

1. seeks information related to various dimensions of personal well-being, such as career interests, community involvement, health matters, and recreational pursuits;

2. designs, develops, and evaluates information products and solutions related to personal interests.

Standard 5: Appreciates and enjoys literature and other creative expressions of information, as described by the following indicators:

1. is a competent and self-motivated reader;
2. derives meaning from information presented creatively in a variety of formats;
3. develops creative products in a variety of formats.

Standard 6: Strives for excellence in information seeking and knowledge generation, as described by the following indicators:

1. assesses the quality of the process and products of one's own information seeking;
2. devises strategies for revising, improving, and updating self-generated knowledge.

Category III: Social Responsibility
The student who contributes positively to the learning community and to society is information literate and:

Standard 7: Recognizes the importance of information to a democratic society, as described by the following indicators:

1. seeks information from diverse sources, contexts, disciplines, and cultures;
2. respects the principle of equitable access to information.

Standard 8: Practices ethical behavior in regard to information and information technology, as described by the following indicators:

1. respects the principles of intellectual freedom;
2. respects intellectual property rights;
3. uses information technology responsibly.

Standard 9: Participates effectively in groups to pursue and generate information, as described by the following indicators:

1. shares knowledge and information with others;
2. respects others' ideas and backgrounds and acknowledges their contributions;
3. collaborates with others, both in person and through technologies, to identify information problems and to seek their solutions;
4. collaborates with others, both in person and through technologies, to design, develop, and evaluate information products and solutions.[32]

Reprinted with permission of the American Library Association and the Association for Educational Communications and Technology, copyright © 1996.

Imagine what academic life would be like if students one day would actually meet these standards! Most campuses still have a long way to go. However, the more faculty integrate information resources and technology into the curriculum, the closer students get to actually becoming living, breathing examples of this vision.

Information Age Campuses

What would an Information Age campus look and sound like? If it existed today, would it be instantly recognizable because it was so different from all other campuses? The following slightly adapted excerpt from the final report of the ALA Presidential Committee on Information Literacy paints a vision of campuses that could one day produce information-literate graduates across the board.

> The campus would be more interactive, because students, pursuing questions of personal interest, would be interacting with other students, with faculty, with a vast array of information resources, and with the community at large to a far greater degree than they presently do today. One would expect to find every student engaged in at least one open-ended, long-term quest for an answer to a serious social, scientific, aesthetic, or political problem. Students' quests would involve not only searching print, electronic, and video data, but also interviewing people both on and off campus. As a result, learning would be more self-initiated. There would be more reading of original sources and more extended writing. Both students and faculty would be familiar with the intellectual and emotional demands of asking productive questions, gathering data of all kinds, reducing and synthesizing information, and analyzing, interpreting, and evaluating information in all its forms.
>
> In such an environment, faculty would be coaching and guiding students more and lecturing less. They would have long since discovered that the classroom computer, with its access to the libraries and databases of the world, is a better source of facts than they could ever hope to be. They would have come to see that their major importance lies in their capacity to arouse curiosity and guide it to a satisfactory conclusion, to ask the right questions at the right time, to stir debate and serious discussion, and to be models themselves of thoughtful inquiry.
>
> Faculty would work consistently with librarians, media resource people, and instructional designers both within their departments and in their communities to ensure that student projects and explorations are challenging, interesting, and productive learning experiences in which they can all take pride. It would not be surprising on such a campus to find a student task force exploring an important community issue with a view toward making a public presentation of its findings on cable television or at a news conference. Nor would it be unusual to see the librarian guiding the task force thought its initial questions and its multi-disciplinary, multimedia search—all the way through to its cable or satellite presentation. In such a role, librarians would be valued for their information expertise and their technological know-how. They would lead frequent faculty development workshops and

ensure that the campus was getting the most out of its investment in information technology. . . .

Finally, one would expect such a campus to look and sound different from today's campus. One would see more information technology than is evident today, and it would be important to people not only in itself but also in regard to its capacity to help them solve problems and create knowledge. One would see the fruits of many student projects prominently displayed on the walls and on bookshelves, and one would hear more discussions and debate about substantive, relevant issues. In the gyms, in the halls, in the cafeteria, and certainly in the classroom, one would hear fundamental questions that make information literacy so important: "How do you know that?" and "What evidence do you have for that?" "Who says?" and "How can we find out?"[33]

CONCLUSION

As the academic leaders at each institution of higher learning realize the vital need for their students to be information literate, their support can facilitate their campuses' entrance into the Information Age with confidence, hope, and excitement. These institutions as a group will then become the "center that holds" as information threatens to spin everything out of control.

The challenge for everyone involved in higher education should be to develop better ways to guide students through the old and new resources as they undertake their search for knowledge in a world and an economy that have changed drastically in just decades. Only through such well-planned leadership is it likely that college graduates will ever develop the full range of abilities that will be absolutely necessary for their future professional flexibility and successful citizenship, and these same graduates will be responsible for keeping the international position of the United States strong and competitive throughout the twenty-first century. The rest of this book is about that challenge.

NOTES

Epigraph: Steven M. Schneider, "Managing the Information Tide: The Human Use of the New Media," *The Annual Review* (1990), 59.

1.   James B. Appleberry, "Changes in Our Future: How Will We Cope?," Faculty speech presented at California State University, Long Beach, CA, August 28, 1992.

2.   Ernest L. Boyer, *College: The Undergraduate Experience in America* (New York: Harper & Row, 1987), 160.

3.   Ibid., 165.

4.   American Library Association, ALA *Presidential Committee on Information Literacy: Final Report* (Chicago: American Library Association, 1989), 7.

5.   Harvie Branscomb, *Teaching with Books: A Study of College Libraries* (Chicago: Association of American Colleges, American Library Association, 1940), 62-63.

6. Frank Newman, *Higher Education and the American Resurgence*, (Princeton, NJ: Princeton University Press, 1985), citing "A Higher Education Agenda for the 99th Congress," 1953, 9-10.

7. Boyer, *College: The Undergraduate Experience*, 160.

8. Patricia Senn Breivik and Robert Wedgeworth, *Libraries and the Search for Academic Excellence* (Metuchen, NJ: Scarecrow Press, 1988), 187-88.

9. American Library Association, *ALA Presidential Committee on Information Literacy: Final Report*, 1.

10. Howard L. Simmons, "Information Literacy and Accreditation: A Middle States Association Perspective," *Information Literacy: Developing Students as Independent Learners, New Directions for Higher Education*, No. 78, edited by D. W. Farmer and Terrance F. Mech (San Francisco: Jossey-Bass, Summer 1992), 15-18.

11. The Commission on Higher Education of the Middle States Association of Colleges and Schools, *Framework for Outcomes Assessment* (Philadelphia: Visual Arts Press, 1990).

12. The Commission on Higher Education of the Middle States Association of Colleges and Schools, *Framework for Outcomes Assessment* (Philadelphia: Visual Arts Press, 1996), 35-36.

13. Ralph A. Wolff, "Using the Accreditation Process to Transform the Mission of the Library," *Information Technology and the Remaking of the University Library, New Directions for Higher Education*, Vol. 90, edited by Beverly Lynch (San Francisco: Jossey-Bass Publishers, Summer 1995), 84-85.

14. "Information Competency: An Initiative for Integrated Learning," position paper, Washington State Community Colleges, 1993.

15. Memo to the Library Media/Directors Council from Ken Hildebrant, chair of the Washington Association of Community and Technical Colleges Instruction Commission, October 27, 1993.

16. Lorie Roth, "Information Competence: How Close Are We?" paper presented at the Conference of the California Community Colleges, San Jose, CA, March 29, 1996, 4.

17. Ibid., 5-6.

18. *Request for Applications—FII/USSP/IJFP/MCHS/METP*, 1997–98, Board of Governors, California Community Colleges Curriculum Services and Instructional Resources Division, 4-5.

19. *Information Competency in the California Community Colleges: A Status Report*, Chancellor's Office staff report to the Educational Policy Committee of the Board of Governors, March 13, 1996.

20. Middle States Association of Colleges and Schools, Commission on Higher Education, *Information Literacy: Lifelong Learning in the Middle States Region: A Summary of Two Symposia*, Philadelphia, March 27, 1995, and Rochester, NY, May 2, 1995.

21. Hannelore B. Radar, "User Education and Information Literacy for the Next Decade: An International Perspective," *Reference Services Review* (Summer 1996), 71-74.

22. *Developing Lifelong Learners Through Undergraduate Education*, Commissioned Report No. 28, National Board of Employment, Education and Training, edited by Philip C. Candy, Gary Crebert, and Jane O'Leary (Australian Government Publishing Service, August, 1994), iii.

23. Ibid.

24. Ibid.

25. Irene Doskatsch, University of South Australia, e-mail to author on March 21, 1997.

26. Shirley J. Behrens, "A Conceptual Analysis and Historical Overview of Information Literacy," *College & Research Libraries*, 55 (July 1994).

27. *INFOLIT: Annual Report*, July 1, 1995 - June 30, 1996 (Cape Town, South Africa, August, 1996), 1.

28. Ping Fang and Daniel Callison, "User Education in Academic Libraries of China," *International Library Review*, 22 (1990), 95-103.

29. Appleberry, "Changes in Our Future," 4.

30. Christine Bruce, Griffith University Information Literacy Blueprint, Division of Information Services, Griffith University, Queensland, Australia, 1994. Also available online at http://www.gu.edu.au/gws/ins/infolit/blueprint.htm.

31. Ibid.

32. For more information on this statement, contact either the American Association of School Librarians, American Library Association, 50 East Huron Street, Chicago, IL 60611 or the Association for Educational Communications and Technology, 1126 16th Street, NW, Washington, DC 20036.

33. American Library Association, ALA *Presidential Committee on Information Literacy: Final Report*, 8-9.

CHAPTER 2

Resource-Based Learning

Knowledge is of two kinds: We know a subject ourselves, or we know where we can find information upon it.

—Dr. Samuel Johnson (1709-1784)

Lorie Roth, director of academic services and professional development at California State University, vividly describes the moment when she first realized what information literacy meant and how important it was for her students.

Amazing as it may seem, I first became concerned about the topic of information literacy by sifting through garbage cans. Before I became a full-time administrator in the Office of the Chancellor at the California State University, I was an English professor. And since English professors are dependent on printed materials for their very livelihood, I have always spent a lot of time in the library. One day, about three years ago, I went to the campus library to get an orientation in the use of computer databases. Our library had just installed one of those giant towers of CD that contained indexes to the humanities, the social sciences, and other disciplines, so I went to the library to get trained in how to use them.

As the librarian explained to me the features of computerized information retrieval, she launched into a complaint that students did not have the skills they needed to be able to use the databases. She then reached into the trash can beside her and pulled out a fistful of computer print-outs. . . . The print-outs recorded every decision made by the students as they conducted the computerized library research—as well as the result of that decision.

As I examined these vestiges of the students' work—and gained glimpses of the thought processes that lay behind this tangible evidence of their skills—I was disheartened more profoundly than I ever before had been in my career. For it was absolutely clear to me that the students who had been sitting at these terminals, these college students who were conducting library research—didn't have the faintest idea of what they were doing. They made every mistake possible. If they were looking for articles about comets, they looked in the Humanities Index, not the Science Index. If they were asked for the name of an author, they typed in "Huckleberry Finn" instead of Mark Twain. If they needed to find sources about a topic, they typed in a key word that was so broad that it generated a list of 657 sources to consult. Or else they typed in a key word like "Flemish tapestry" and were surprised that the computer turned up no entries at all. They searched haphazardly, moving from using a keyword like "animal" to a phrase like "Chanel perfume" or the "War of 1812."

As I sat there, surrounded by the detritus from the trash cans, paging through these print-outs, I tried to reconstruct what kind of thought processes these students were using. I finally arrived at the conclusion that, in fact, there was no process; that there was no logical, clear, systematic inquiry; that the students at my university did not, in fact, have the skills necessary to find the information they needed. And I thought that I as a teacher had failed, and that we as a collective faculty had not done right by our students by allowing them to be information illiterates in the Age of Information.

There before me on the table I had tangible evidence that students did not know how to find information. If they didn't know how to find it, could I have any confidence that they knew how to evaluate the information? Or how to use the information in a responsible manner? That's when I became a convert, on the spot—not even just a convert, but more like a zealot—on the topic of information competence—and how important it is for survival in today's world.[1]

If this current generation of students is ever going to be information literate—if they are ever going to be successful leaders in the next century—academicians must stop assuming that students know how to research information, or that students can easily learn research skills without any intervention. By finding new and different ways to approach learning, academic leaders must make certain that students are prepared to face the challenges of a constantly expanding flood of information.

THE LIMITATIONS OF LECTURE

Research documenting the limitations of lectures as a means of learning has already led some colleges and universities to acknowledge the need for substantive reform in the teaching/learning process. For example, the following summary of research from *Redesigning Higher Education*, a 1994 ASHE-ERIC Higher Education Report, leaves little doubt that classroom business-as-usual cannot be tolerated on campuses that place a high value on student learning.

How much do they [students] remember? Studies of the retention of course material (Gustav 1969; McLeish 1968) at all levels of schooling generally show rare high values of as much as 50 percent retained, but results frequently drop below 20 percent (Brethower 1977). The published values for remembering are probably overestimates, as the student has often forgotten some information by the time the initial measurements are taken and presumably will continue to do so after the final post-test (Brethower 1977).

One carefully designed study at Norwich (England) University tested students almost immediately following a specially designed lecture (McLeish 1969). Students were tested on their recall of facts, theory, and application of content they had just heard, and they were allowed maximum use of the lecture notes they had just taken, knowing they would be tested, and a printed summary of the lecture. The average for students' recall of this information was only 42 percent. One week later, a subgroup of these students was retested with the same test they had already taken, presumably making them beneficiaries of test practice effects. Although recall among the students varied (with some remembering three times as much as others), they remembered an average of only 20 percent of the lecture content, having forgotten in one week an additional 50 percent of what they had remembered earlier from the lecture. A second study of Northern Polytechnic University architecture students also found that students recalled only 42 percent of a lecture's content when tested almost immediately after the lecture (McLeish 1968).

"In general, very little of a lecture can be recalled except in the case of listeners with above-average education and intelligence" (Verner and Dickinson, cited in Bonwell and Eison 1991, p. 9). "Given the placement scores of many freshmen, this statement should give pause to most instructors in higher education" (p. 9). One can only imagine the effect on current students of what has become the Lecture System. If higher-order thinking skills "are retained and used long after the individual has forgotten the detailed specifics of the subject matter taught in schools" (Bloom 1984, p. 14) and if, as the old adage suggests, education is what remains after the facts are forgotten, what does the accumulated research reviewed here imply for the quality of our graduates? Would it not be wiser to focus less on facts and more on developing these higher-order skills?[2]

RESOURCE-BASED LEARNING

As a result of such irrefutable research, a growing number of campuses are offering students the opportunity to take a new active role in their own education, to move away from their traditional passive role as receptacles for information supplied by professors. In their new role, students are assuming responsibility for identifying and securing information for problems and needs, and then often for taking concrete action based on that information.

Responding to this shift in student learning, many schools and universities are already actively seeking and employing the following strategies to support an active undergraduate learning environment that will prepare their students for lifelong learning and problem solving:

- undergraduate research
- service learning
- inquiry learning
- problem-based learning
- evidence-based learning

Although these efforts have different names, they are not as estranged from one another as they may seem because they all rest on the foundation of *resource-based learning,* which is the basis for student achievement of information literacy.

Resource-based learning is a commonsense approach to learning. If students are to continue learning throughout their lives, they must be able to access, evaluate, organize, and present information from all the real-world sources existing in today's information society. Such sources include books, journals, television, online databases, radio, community experts, government agencies, the Internet, and CD-ROMs. As a result, all these sources become learning tools.

Resource-based learning usually produces a result, or outcome, that is more tangible and varied than the writing of a term paper or the delivering of a class speech. A few of the many possible outcomes include serving a community by researching an existing community problem and documenting the possible solutions, developing a World Wide Web (WWW) page, and creating a television program or a publication. Such specific outcomes develop students' abilities to systematically and effectively approach new situations, and promote future success through student experiences of real accomplishments that mean more than just a grade. Even more important, students realize practical benefits for themselves; they acquire experience for their resumes and for discussion during their first job interviews.

Resource-based learning also frequently emphasizes teamwork over individual performance. Not only does working in teams allow students to acquire people-related skills and learn how to make the most of their own strengths and weaknesses, but it also parallels the way in which they will need to live and work throughout their lives.

IMPORTANT BENEFITS OF RESOURCE-BASED LEARNING

Resource-based learning usually results in two important student benefits: it prepares students for lifelong learning, and it allows them to achieve greater academic success because it makes provision for the differences in students' learning needs and abilities.

Lifelong Learning

First and foremost, resource-based learning prepares students for lifelong learning beyond the classroom; to achieve information literacy, students must be given repeated opportunities to work with the same information resources that will bombard them throughout their lives. To help their students become information literate, faculty—supported by academic librarians and other information specialists—must move away from single-text teaching and focus on exposing students to real-world information resources and technologies. At its best, this process puts the fun back into learning by allowing students to experience the excitement epitomized by the image of a special prosecutor or police detective seeking and sifting through complex issues and even seemingly contradictory facts to reach the truth.

However, resource-based learning is *not* simply providing faculty with a hundred books, five videotapes, three online databases, and two presentations about a certain topic. Instead, the process moves faculty members to spend more time looking at and analyzing the topic, deciding the major issues to be covered in relationship to the topic, and—with the help of information specialists—facilitating students' ability to locate, evaluate, and effectively use resources that will allow them to meet the desired learning objectives of the course. As a result, resource-based learning selectively integrates the resources and services of the library and of the world into daily classroom experiences— along with the exhortation to students to go and do likewise in their own lives.

Academic Success through Individualized Learning

Second, such a wide use of learning resources allows for flexibility in how students learn. When people talk about "the good old days" in education and express the desire to return to them, they largely remember a homogeneous world. In those days, at the K-12 level, students with significant handicaps were not seen in regular classrooms, and IQ tests were used as the primary bases for separating slower learners from brighter ones. Under these circumstances, one textbook, one workbook, and one lesson plan seemed to meet the educational needs of any one classroom of students. As a result, school systems produced a reasonably homogeneous group of college-bound graduates.

However, as everyone knows, "the good old days" have not existed for some time now. Today, classrooms contain students with widely diverse learning abilities and learning styles. Such differences are most easily observed on urban campuses and community colleges where great diversity within the student body is often a given and sometimes a cherished reality. On such campuses, with their exciting mixtures of first-generation, international, honor, and everything-in-between students, it is ludicrous to assume that all students are at the same academic level or that any one teaching/learning approach can meet all their needs.

For years, educators have talked about individualizing the learning process to accommodate different learning styles, and for some time now testing has been able to determine preferred learning styles. But unless resource-based learning is implemented, there is really no practical means—within reasonable budget limitations—of providing the rich variety in learning resources necessary to achieve an individualized approach to learning.

With the necessary support, however, faculty can move their students out into the larger world of the academic library, into the community beyond the campus, and even across international borders. Within this larger universe, students can find information on diverse topics written at their reading levels or packaged in a manner best suited to their own learning styles. For example, common sense dictates that an encyclopedia article or a well-written textbook introduction to a topic will be more helpful for launching most students into a new field of study than the latest scholarly thesis on the topic. But for students whose home and school experiences have not resulted in strong reading comprehension skills, print-only options will always place them at a disadvantage with fellow classmates.

A resource-based learning approach, however, allows students the option of learning from more than one medium. Of course, improving reading levels and creating a desire to read should always be the priorities of every educator, but reading is simply not always the best way for all students to learn all subjects. Furthermore, text alone or text with only minimal pictures does not reflect the normal life experiences of most students today, who spend far more time watching television than reading. Students currently entering college straight from high school are estimated to have watched over 15,000 hours of television. Many of these students could have their understanding of the Civil War greatly enhanced by viewing Ken Burns's excellent 1990 PBS documentary *The Civil War*, by seeing *Gone with the Wind*, by studying a wealth of related multimedia information sources about this era, or by accessing the American Civil War WWW Information Archive at http://WWW.ACCESS.digex.net/~bdboyle/cw.html. Depending on where students live, they could also benefit from observing or even participating in a reenactment of a Civil War battle or from touring actual battle sites. Such a variety of learning resources would accommodate different learning styles and make for a far more interesting course for everyone.

Finally, resource-based learning is more relevant to students' own lives. Most students, for example, can easily relate their everyday worlds to newspapers, television news, the local free net, government publications, and online databases. The importance of perceived relevance can explain, at least in part, research that documents the value of students' involvement in teaching their own classes. For example, as part of the quality teaching project at the University of Texas, instructors in human ecology and mechanical engineering courses "found that students put more effort into their learning when they were responsible for finding resources, mastering the material, and preparing a presentation."[3]

In summary, resource-based learning helps level the playing field for learning. It is a commonsense approach to promoting student success because it eliminates barriers to learning by allowing students to learn from sources with which they are most comfortable, and it increases learning motivation by allowing students to learn from materials that exist in their everyday lives.

CRITICAL THINKING AND RESOURCE-BASED LEARNING

A strong tie exists between resource-based learning and critical thinking. Proponents of both concepts are keenly aware of the need to create healthy skepticism about information provided by mass media or most easily accessed. The old and fascinating literature of fakes and forgeries includes the recent finding of "Hitler's diaries." Although few students will ever be required to authenticate documents, all will need to be wary consumers of information, both on and off line. Early in 1997, for example, researchers at Princeton University offered documentation of a number of deficiencies in the structure of the WWW that made possible the simulation of legitimate sites for purposes of tricking users into giving out credit card numbers and other valuable information.[4] Besides fraud, students need to recognize information produced by propagandists and people with strongly felt biases. Being able to assess the scholarly quality of any information from any source is both a critical thinking and an information literacy goal.

Threasa Wesley, the coordinator of instructional services at Northern Kentucky University, has written a thoughtful article that stresses the need for librarians and faculty to teach students that what they do with information is far more important than where or how they found the information. Wesley believes that an effort should be made to dislodge students' blind faith in information sources, and she suggests some tactics that might be helpful in accomplishing that goal.

> Primarily we want to teach students that scholars and authorities do disagree and that this is a positive catalyst to the creation of new knowledge. A discussion of conflicts among scholars will probably be

surprising to students. Much of the educational process does not make this lack of complete consensus evident: single instructors for a class, straight lecture classes, single texts—all summary type sources that take the edge off the controversy and varying interpretations of any issue.

Secondly, we can show them that factual information is fluid and can change due to its context. For example, some reports claim plastics make up 30% of the landfill while others claim only 8%. Which is true? Why is there a difference? Investigation of the sources cited in these reports indicates that one source is discussing volume, the other weight. Students should know the context of facts before using them in their own analysis of an issue.

Finally, we should try to build students' confidence in their own ability to question and judge the value, relevancy, accuracy, bias, etc., of these information sources.[5]

Those interested in the critical thinking aspects of information literacy should read Craig Gibson's 1995 article "Critical Thinking: Implications for Instruction." Gibson, who is now associate director for information services at George Mason University, not only addresses "the most frequently asked questions about critical thinking as applied to information access-abilities," but also raises some intriguing ideas that deserve serious consideration—such as the potential powerful effect of having students model critical thinking for other students.[6]

One of the best examples of a course that meets the critical thinking/information literacy challenge straight on is at North Park College in Chicago. A collaboration of librarians and English Department faculty resulted in a composition course that teaches the distinction between scholarship and propaganda. The course begins with a brief lecture that defines propaganda and scholarship. Then a student discussion of the differences between the two is followed by a class analysis of an article from a scholarly work that examines the use of propaganda by Americans and Japanese during World War II.

The class is then divided into groups of four, and each group is given subject matter from a different point of view that has been found in news articles, scholarly journals, and popular magazines from World War II. The groups analyze the articles, summarize their findings, and present oral reports to the class. The second assignment, which consists of further group collaboration on different aspects of propaganda, is followed up with the production of 10-page literature reviews. When all the work is completed, the students select one aspect of their group project about which they want to conduct further research. That research results in their final assignment, a 15-page research paper based on an analysis of their findings.[7]

Not only does it make sense that critical thinking skills and resource-based learning go hand-in-hand, but this intrinsically related duo is also practical: Students will automatically acquire or sharpen their critical thinking skills as they become information literate through resource-based learning programs.

COLLABORATION

Collaboration, especially between classroom faculty and librarians, is essential to the success of resource-based learning (instructional designers and media and academic computer staff can also be valuable additions to instructional team efforts). Unfortunately, librarians at many research universities are seen as second-class citizens or handmaidens to the faculty, a situation that creates a particular challenge in the development of resource-based learning programs or projects. On the other hand, faculty at community and liberal arts colleges more frequently view librarians as partners in a teaching/learning team.

Because no scholar/teacher can keep up with all information resources and technologies, campuses must recognize the particular subject expertise of librarians, i.e., expertese regarding the organization of information and how to access and evaluate it across all formats and technologies. The 1995 California State University (CSU) systemwide workshop found "real evidence of productive synergy when cooperation of discipline and library faculty occurs."[8] However, at CSU and many other campuses, "most of the time discipline and library faculty exist in separate and distinct spheres, and there are no incentives or rewards to encourage collaboration."[9] Often such attitudes are reinforced by campus restrictions on librarians' involvement with instruction-related committees or by librarians' ineligibility to obtain teaching grants. Failure to make the director of libraries an active member of the deans' council or its equivalent can also reinforce this unproductive mind set.

The Commission on Higher Education (CHE) of the Middle States Association of Colleges and Schools has been encouraging information literacy on campuses for years. The title of a 1996 speech by Oswald M.T. Ratteray, assistant director of the Commission, best reflects the importance of collaboration efforts between faculty members and librarians: "Faculty and Librarians: Twin Pillars of Information Literacy: Instruction and Evaluation."[10] In his speech, Ratteray highlights six questions as "the building blocks for inquiry into information literacy during the self-study process" and for visiting teams to address in the accreditation process. The importance of faculty and librarian collaboration is underscored in three of the six questions.

- To what extent are faculty and librarians recognized as twin pillars in information literacy instruction and evaluation? In other words, does the entire campus community recognize the significance of information literacy in all aspects of the curriculum, its centrality to teaching and learning, and its role in demonstrating institutional improvement?

- If learning (of information literacy skills) has not occurred or if insufficient learning has occurred, have faculty and librarians individually utilized the data to improve their joint and separate teaching responsibilities?

- Do faculty and librarians participate in institution-wide committees to ensure coherence in the information literacy program within and among various disciplines and departmental levels?

The shift of focus from teaching to learning makes librarians and other information providers and instructional specialists important and necessary contributors to the learning environment. For example, as part of a thoughtful two-part 1994 *Change* article on restructuring universities, Alan E. Guskin, chancellor of the five-campus Antioch University, urged a three-pronged learning strategy that considers what students can best learn independently or with peers through technology and what requires their interaction with faculty. In regard to learning through technology, Guskin states, "A major faculty role, and especially the role of the librarian as information technology expert, will be to guide students to these sources by helping them learn how to ask the right questions."[11]

In another *Change* article in 1995, William M. Plater, dean of the faculties and executive vice chancellor at Indiana University-Purdue University in Indianapolis, looked at the future work of faculty and offered a "provocative and imaginative" list for managing faculty time more efficiently. Among the items listed, two lend particular support to the kind of partnerships that are needed for successful information literacy programs.

- Expand the variety and types of faculty roles and appointments to include librarians, clinicians, practitioners, professionals, and technicians as members of a team with shared goals.

- Authorize faculty and staff to support independent student learners in a model of decentralized interaction based on established outcomes for both parties.[12]

The very number of calls for rethinking the teaching/learning process underscores the fact that most campuses have a long way to go. Only so far as academic leaders can gain serious faculty commitment to focusing on student learning and only insofar as faculty are willing to work collaboratively with librarians will the campus environment allow programs of information literacy to flourish.

CONCLUSION

Resource-based learning is a commonsense approach to addressing the diversity of student abilities present in any class. Such differences are accommodated by allowing students, with the guidance of faculty and librarians, to find and learn from materials that are at their comprehension levels and in formats that match their preferred learning styles. In addition, resource-based learning offers students increased motivation to learn because the materials are relevant to their out-of-school lives, and, most of all, this approach to learning prepares today's young people for lifelong learning by providing them with opportunities to become savvy information consumers.

NOTES

1. Lorie Roth, "Information Competency: How Close Are We?" A Panel Presentation on Working Together for Student Success, Conference at the California Community Colleges, San Jose, CA, March 29, 1996, 1-3.

2. Lion Gardiner, *Redesigning Higher Education: Producing Dramatic Gains in Student Learning*, ASHE-ERIC Higher Education Report, No. 7 (Washington, DC: Graduate School of Education and Human Development, The George Washington University, 1994), 46-47. The studies cited in this quote include the following:

    B.S. Bloom, "The Search for Methods of Group Intervention as Effective One-to-One Tutoring," *Educational Leadership*, 41 (1984), 4-17.

    C.C. Bonwell and J.A. Eison, *Active Learning: Creating Excitement in the Classroom*, ASHE-ERIC Higher Education Report, No. 1 (Washington, DC: George Washington University, School of Education and Human Development, 1991), ED336 049, 121, MF-01; PG-05.

    D.M. Brethower, "Recent Research in Learning Behavior: Some Implications for College Teaching," *Teaching in Higher Education*, edited by S. Scholl and R.S. Inglis (Columbus, OH: Ohio Board of Regents, 1977).

    A. Gustav, "Retention of Course Material after Varying Intervals of Time," *Psychological Reports*, 25 (1969), 727-30.

    J. McLeish, *The Lecture Method* (Cambridge: Cambridge Institute of Education, 1968).

3. Marilla Svinicki and Michelle O'Reilly, "When Faculty Try Quality," *AAHE Bulletin*, 49 (November, 1996), 11.

4. Jeffrey R. Young, and David L. Wilson, "Researchers Warn of the Ease with which Fake Web Pages Can Fool Internet Users," *The Chronicle of Higher Education*, XLLIII, No. 18 (January 10, 1997), A25.

5. Threasa Wesley, "Teaching Library Research: Are We Preparing Students for Effective Information Use?" *Emergency Librarian*, 18 (January/February, 1991), 29-30.

6. Lori Arp, ed., "Library Literacy," *RQ*, 35, No. 1 (Fall, 1995), 27-35.

7. Sonia Bodi, "Scholarship or Propaganda: How Can Librarians Help Undergraduates Tell the Difference?" *The Journal of Academic Librarianship*, 21 (January, 1995), 21-25.

8. "Information Competence in the CSU: A Report," submitted by Work Group on Information Competence to the Commission on Learning Resources and Instructional Technology [photocopy], California State University, Long Beach, CA, December, 1995, 14.

9. Ibid.

10. Oswald M.T. Ratteray, "Faculty and Librarians: Twin Pillars of Information Literacy: Instruction and Evaluation," a speech presented at a session on "The Future of College Libraries," Wartburg College, Waverly, IA, October 15, 1996, 5-6.

11. Alan E. Guskin, "Reducing Student Costs & Enhancing Student Learning: Restructuring the Role of Faculty," *Change,* 26, No. 5 (September, 1994), 21.

12. William M. Plater, "Future Work: Faculty Time in the 21st Century," *Change,* 27, No. 3 (May/June, 1995), 32-33.

CHAPTER 3

Successful Information Literacy Programs

Information literacy is needed to guarantee the survival of democratic institutions.

—U.S. Representative Major Owens, 1976

This chapter might seem the perfect place to lay out a simple formula or set of guidelines for establishing successful resource-based learning efforts that would guarantee that all currently enrolled students are information literate when they graduate. Common sense, however, suggests that the diversity of the 3,000-plus campuses in the United States will require modifications to any program to meet the special needs and requirements of each and every mission and student body. For example, the developers of the program at the U.S. Coast Guard Academy have a major planning advantage because they are planning for a more homogenous student body than the ones existing on most campuses. In addition, the focused educational program itself allows information-literacy efforts at the Academy to ensure a progression of learning skills over the four years from specific research tools the first year to the mastery of information evaluation abilities in later years. Few other campuses could use such a singularly structured approach.[1]

However, some insights can be gleaned from the many past information-literacy efforts to save campuses from experimenting with approaches that have consistently failed. These insights can also provide some guidance in the process of planning successful information-literacy programs. This chapter, therefore, will describe such plans and strategies as they relate specifically to general education and overall planning. These descriptions will provide a series of snapshots of resource-based learning in action. Chapter 4 will cover a series of subject-specific models that will be useful for college and departmental planning.

ALTERNATIVES TO THE STATUS QUO

Educators interested in preparing their students for life in the Information Age need to stand back and take a fresh look at the status quo—at everything from term papers to typical general education requirements. Then they need to ask this question: Is business-as-usual producing active learners who will be prepared for lifelong learning in the twenty-first century?

Term Papers

The traditional term paper is a common student experience on all campuses. Unfortunately, this standard bearer of education, which is usually given heavy weight in the overall course grade, does little to develop students' research skills because it does not require students to consider the body of existing information on a topic. Instead, students simply can—and usually do—pull together just enough "at random" information to support the requirements of the paper. Students' patterns of gathering and using information today are certainly in keeping with the ideas expressed in the 1980s by Harlan Cleveland, the former dean of the University of Minnesota's Hubert Humphrey Institute of Public Affairs, who said that information, unlike other commodities, is never wanted in any greater quantity than is needed for the issue or decision at hand.[2]

Typically, when students search for information, they settle on the most easily acquired information, and they cease collecting data when the required number of sources has been located. Most students, due to inadequate guidance, have little concern for how much information really exists on their topic, for how wide the range of perspectives is on the topic, or for what the most reliable, authoritative, and up-to-date information on the topic may be. What's more, online databases, CD-ROMs, and the Internet, all touted as the current end-all of information technology, are not leading to any better research. Most students are content with whatever materializes from their first few keystrokes.

Although seemingly ingrained in students and professors alike, this approach to a term paper assignment can be transformed into a learning experience that requires students to become more deliberate about their use of information resources and helps them develop their information literacy abilities. By far the easiest adaptation of the traditional term paper is to continue to assign it during the first class period but to provide a timetable that runs throughout the semester for turning in progressive steps in the development of the paper. This plan can be easily accomplished by simply having a timetable—such as the following—built into course syllabi.

Session 1:	Paper assigned.
Session 3:	Topic statements due. (Check for topic feasibility: Is the focus too broad or too narrow? Does a reasonable body of information exist on the topic?)
Session 5:	Annotated bibliographies due. (Check for appropriateness of research: Is it adequate for the topic? Are the resources authoritative and timely?)
Session 7:	Outline of paper due with references included where they will be used. (Check for organization: Does the thought process seem to progress logically? Is there adequate research to support the key issues?)
Session 8:	First draft of paper due. (Check for thought development: Is the theme well developed? Do the references support the theme?)
Sessions 9-11:	Opportunities to rewrite papers.
Session 12:	Final papers due.
Session(s) 14 (15):	Selected papers shared and discussed by class. (Reinforce assignment by using examples of good thought development and good supporting research.)

This generic model for assigning term papers can be modified to match the literature of a particular discipline. For example, Appendix D reproduces a detailed syllabus from an intensive writing course within the psychology program at Wheaton College in Massachusetts. The course is designed to teach students how to write a literature review paper, and the introduction to the assignment underscores for students the value of such a learning approach whenever a topic needs to be researched thoroughly, even after college.

This approach to term papers offers an excellent opportunity for collaboration among students, faculty, and librarians. When they get involved with students early in such courses, librarians are able to provide help and direction toward ensuring that each student's individual developmental research needs are addressed. Librarians are also particularly helpful in assessing the students' annotated bibliographies and the appropriateness of their use in the development of student papers.

This interaction with librarians is essential because students will inevitably exhibit various levels of abilities and experience with research skills, and custom-tailored exposure to the research process and to the evaluation of information resources can greatly enhance research skills. The emphasis is on custom-tailored exposure because the traditional one-period library session—in which students are supposed to learn, as a group, about every research tool that exists for a particular subject area—is inadequate at best.

As an alternative, faculty can work with campus librarians to explore other options and possibilities—such as holding one or more classes in the library when the students are actually beginning to research their papers. During those sessions, the students could be divided into small groups based upon the topics they have chosen. The faculty member could discuss useful background information with one group; the librarian could discuss particular research possibilities with another group; and a third group could actually begin to research. Whatever approach is taken to help students master research skills, it should later be evaluated to enhance future efforts.

Another method of helping students master research skills that has worked successfully on a number of campuses is to have professors provide a truly good piece of scholarly writing for use as a model that students can emulate. This method is used within a number of disciplines at Western Washington University where it is called "running backwards from the finish line."[3] In this approach, a professor spends time with the students exploring what makes the selected piece of writing such a good paper; the class examines the documented research, looks for evidence of critical thinking and thought development, and analyzes what makes the writing clear and readable. Such specific attention helps students internalize scholarly expectations and become better researchers. Such modelling, if done in more than one discipline, also helps students understand how standards, procedures, and expectations differ from one discipline to another.

Once again, the collaboration of librarians in such sessions can enhance learning outcomes because they can offer expert guidance on how to evaluate the documentation and can show how it fits into the available literature of the field. Students benefit greatly from personally understanding their professors' expectations for quality and from seeing, perhaps for the first time, the potential value of information specialists to the research process.

John Lanning, a chemistry professor at the University of Colorado at Denver and an early proponent of writing across the curriculum, also became an early champion of information literacy across the curriculum. In addressing a group of academic librarians about his experience with team teaching a chemistry literature course with a librarian, Lanning told his audience that his students' most important learning experience came from seeing the librarian learning from him and from seeing him learn from the librarian.[4] His students learned a lot about the need for lifelong learning and the value of partnering with information specialists in the research process.

Small Group Assignments

Many of the existing alternatives to the traditional term paper are designed to increase students' mastery of research skills. Before considering any alternatives, a professor must first consider the purpose of the assignment within the context of the course. If the purpose is to develop writing skills, then written assignments are necessary. However, if the purpose is for students to develop critical thinking skills, learn about the literature of the field, or gain subject knowledge, then alternatives to a term paper assignment are more attractive.

Substituting a debate or a debate-like approach for a writing assignment, for example, can be effective in reinforcing information literacy and critical thinking skills. Students not only have to research their point of view, but they also need to research the opposing view to be prepared for any attacks on their arguments. At Wayne State University in Detroit, a required, one-credit freshman "survival course" has been completely redesigned to use a debate approach that has small teams take opposing sides on topics of current interest. The rationale developed for the new course includes the following:

> In today's Information Society, learning how to find and manage information enables students to succeed in their studies, in lifelong learning, and in decision making. The right information at the right time equals power. The sooner students tap into that power, the better things will be for them, and UGE 100 is designed to put the students in the driver's seat for the Information Highway. . . .
>
> In UGE 100 students will gain experience in identifying information needed for a particular assignment and will learn effective ways to locate the information they need. They will also gain experience in evaluating how good the information is, and in learning how to put good information to work for them in order to prove a point and get people to pay attention to their ideas. . . . All team members will be responsible for doing their share in bringing together the information ammunition needed to effectively arm their team for both presenting their case and for defending their position against the attacks of the other team.[5]

Doing research for a debate is intrinsically more adventuresome than doing research for "just another paper" because students know they will need to verbally answer challenges to their research. Moreover, debate teams provide for small group interaction that enriches the interpersonal learning aspects of the research.

In another highly stimulating activity, students are assigned to small groups to develop a case for changing some situation that will convince one or more decision-makers. For example, they might try to make a convincing argument for the protection of a certain endangered species, the importance of continuing space exploration, or the legality of assisted suicide. During timed presentations, the rest of the class and the instructor serve as the person(s) to be influenced. Besides requiring resource-based learning, this discovery approach to learning simulates work and community service situations that almost always involve a group of people working together to solve a problem by swaying opinion. In addition, the students' experiences parallel the experiences of legislators and others by exposing the students to "diversity, chaos, conflicting expertise, and [a] focus on community viability."[6]

Several institutions in the state of Washington use an approach that is similar to this team approach to discovery learning.

> The basic unit of instruction is the 16-credit problem-focused learning community. Two to four professors work together (frequently with librarians as team members) with students to find the answer to some problem for which the solution is not known beforehand. That is what the real world is like. We have to create a context in our institutions of higher education in which people of diverse perspectives, backgrounds, colors, genders, and countries are working together to solve problems to which the answer is not known at the beginning.[7]

Another creative variation on teamwork is to have groups of students reinvent different events in history. For example, one group of students could research the Civil War period and construct a scenario discussing what would have happened if General Lee had not surrendered at Appomattox; another group could explore how the *Titanic*'s survival would have changed history. Such research challenges draw more than average interest from students and could be used in a number of disciplines. Usually the results are successful because students have an opportunity to combine their brains with their imaginations, and the literature on how people learn is clear that more learning occurs when students enjoy their work.

For any of the above activities to provide an effective means by which students can master information literacy skills, the criteria for student evaluations must be clearly defined to emphasize the research aspects of the assignments rather than the presentation. Such an evaluation might require an annotated bibliography to be completed sometime before the debate or presentation. In addition, any assessment should include an evaluation of the appropriateness and thoroughness of the information that was gathered and of how that information was used and presented.

Stand-Alone Research Courses

At first glance, a whole course on research skills may appear extremely beneficial because such a course affords enough time to ensure adequate coverage of material. Unfortunately, stand-alone elective courses—even when offered for credit—seldom attract many students. For example, Montana State University recently updated one of its two-credit traditional research courses to cover electronic information. The course emphasizes class discussions and collaborative group problem solving, and focuses on the critical/valuative aspects of information literacy and on key but nonsubject-specific resources (e.g., electronic resources, statistical information, government documents).[8] Although interest seems to be growing, the highest number of students to ever sign up for the course in one semester is 24.

Hoping to provide for the skills that students need, California State University, San Jose offered a course entitled "Library 20 Introduction to Computing for Personal Information Management." In the catalog, the three-unit class is described as an "Introduction to computing for personal information access, use, and management, including basic computer operations, access to geographically distributed information on the global Internet, electronic communication, word processing and document design, data modeling with spreadsheets, database design and maintenance for information storage and retrieval, and information presentation."[9] The campus student newspaper carried the following advertisement for the course:

> Need valuable computer skills for tomorrow's work place? "Home page" design, spreadsheets, image design, databases, information presentation, word processing, data modeling, UNIX, Internet skills. Want an exciting course for Spring 1997?? Then check this out!![10]

Although this course does not begin to develop the critical thinking skills usually associated with courses designed to develop more traditional research skills, its focus was expected to be more effective than more traditional research courses in drawing students. That was not the case. The course's enrollment has always been low—six at tops.

However, a third type of general education information literacy course is emerging. It complements—but does not replace—the learning that takes place in courses like those at Montana State and California State at San Jose. The Graduate School of Library and Information Science at the University of California at Berkeley offers undergraduates an example of this new type of course. The Berkeley course deals with the social implications of today's Information Age. Entitled "Information Systems," this course was developed as one of the two foundation courses for an undergraduate liberal arts minor in library and information science. Course designer Michael Buckland describes the course as follows:

> The class explores what various notions of "information" and "information system" might include: the social, political and economic aspects of information management and information technology, and so on. Privacy issues and the discovery that information systems have a cultural basis consistently arouse interest. Students are surprised by how widely the meaning of the word "information" varies from one context to another. Exploration of the characteristics of retrieval systems includes exercises that do result in useful skills, but utility is not the primary intent.[11]

Commenting on student expectations for the course, Buckland said:

> Students have very little basis for knowing what to expect of such a course. Most expect a utilitarian class that will teach them how to search in online retrieval systems. . . . The idea that there already is a

rich, complex and interesting field to be explored concerning information, how it is managed, and how it influences daily life, is ordinarily absent.[12]

As good as any such credited courses may be, the important questions to ask are the following:

- How many students will squeeze such a course into their schedules as a general education elective?
- Will faculty believe that such a course is important enough to encourage students to enroll?
- How does such a course fit into the overall information literacy planning across the curriculum?

Can anything be done to make basic information literacy courses more effective in reaching students? One solution is making a research course part of the general education requirements. One example of this approach has been in place at the University of Michigan since January 1991. Sophomores in the College of Literature, Science, and the Arts Honors Program are required to take a seminar in which they must work closely with a faculty member to develop a piece of substantive writing that exhibits critical thinking and analytic skills. Librarian Barbara MacAdam credits the students with some of the content and the name of the course, which currently is "Knowledge and Society in the Information Age." MacAdam says that her challenge "is to push students to think about ideas and questions that push their thinking to a level and substance beyond what they learn from mass media."[13] The following description for this University of Michigan course covers many issues and aspects of the Information Age:

What do the following ideas have in common?

- virtual reality
- censorship
- free speech
- intellectual property
- information ethics
- hyperspace

- right to privacy
- intellectual freedom
- information overload
- morphing
- bias in information transfer
- information economics

Designed to provide students with a better understanding of the complexities and implications of our knowledge-based society, this course will investigate the ways in which everyday lives and methods of scholarly investigation have been profoundly altered by technology and the information explosion. Through readings, class discussions and papers, students will have the opportunity to explore selected information issues in depth, and will develop an understanding of the comparative methods of inquiry and knowledge dissemination within and across the sciences, arts, and social science disciplines.[14]

Another way to enhance the value of information literacy courses is to link them to a subject course. For instance, a research course and an English composition course can easily be linked together. Shelton State Community College (Alabama) offers a good example that also involves a "linkage" with a nearby university library.

At Shelton, all students enrolled in English Composition I and II are concurrently required to be enrolled, respectively, in the one-credit courses entitled "Library Skills" and "Research Skills." The basic orientation and skills development components serve as a basis for the second library or research course that focuses on learning more sophisticated search techniques, such as keyword searching, and on the use of specialized indexes or collections, such as Government Documents (available at University of Alabama Libraries but not at Shelton State Library). Because the latter course is designed to help students learn how to gather information and develop a research strategy for research papers, students seem to be particularly receptive to the University of Alabama component of the course.[15]

Seattle Central Community College also offers a five-credit English composition course and a three-credit library course that are linked around the theme of cultural pluralism. The faculty and librarians plan as a team and teach back-to-back during the two-hour class meetings. The courses are advertised to students under the heading: "Thinking as a Writer, Thinking as a Researcher—Putting It All Together."[16] Assignments in the class are based on the following conceptual framework:

> Learning as process; problem solving; critical questions; strategies for writing by focusing on audience, occasion and purpose; strategies for research by developing the ability to recognize and use information systems; logic of information and documentation systems; use of the computer for inventing and generating topics and for writing, editing and information retrieval; learning communities; and nontraditional assessments of student learning. Using this framework, faculty and librarians planned the linked courses according to a common outline: (1) Cultural Pluralism and the Power of Information, (2) Academic Disciplines and the Classification of Knowledge, (3) Evaluation of Information Resources, (4) Computers and Research, and (5) The Right to Information and How to Protect It. . . .
>
> Instructors design assignments using multicultural themes and concepts in all units. Students are encouraged, but not required, to choose topics on cultural pluralism. Examples of past topics chosen by students are "Black Politicians: A Comparison of Marcus Garvey and Malcolm X," "The Influence of Japanese Art on Impressionism," and "Deaf Culture in America." The practice of showing students sample information formats is one of the easiest ways to integrate cultural pluralism.[17]

Weber State University in Ogden, Utah, developed a unique prototype that links three disciplines: economics, computer science, and library science.

In this particular model, students are given coordinated assignments among all three disciplines that require them to use skills they gained in each course. The faculty and librarians grade assignments collaboratively, and they meet regularly to evaluate student progress and discuss teaching techniques.[18]

Whatever the subject area, linked courses allow students to observe faculty and librarian coordination and cooperation, and require students to apply research and computer skills to a content course. As a result, students can more easily understand the real value of these skills for their future academic and career success.

PLANNING STRATEGIES

A chief weakness of all the approaches described so far in this chapter is their failure to fit into any overall curriculum planning for information literacy. Indeed, the great majority of campus information literacy efforts to date have been largely ad hoc in nature. Although innovative courses are being offered on many campuses today, the majority are isolated endeavors that do not begin to ensure that all the students—or even half the students—will acquire essential information literacy abilities.

The most effective way to ensure that all students will be information literate when they graduate is to devise a well-conceived campus strategy in which subject-specific efforts build upon a foundation of research skills mastered as part of general education or core curriculum offerings. A helpful parallel is writing across the curriculum. The history of this movement provides insight into what does and does not work well. In a 1988 speech, Deborah Hatch, writing consultant for the Center for Instructional Development and Research at the University of Washington, expertly summed up the movement's three generations, or stages, of development.

- writing centered in English courses
- collaboration of writing and discipline-based faculty
- writing faculty member as a facilitator or consultant to discipline-based faculty

If resource-based learning is to be truly successful, all librarians will ultimately have to move beyond the collaborative teaching stage to a consultant-type role. Hatch suggests that at this consultant level of interaction, librarians will view their expertise with information resources and technology "as secondary to the course goals and teaching strategies of their colleagues in other disciplines"; librarians will begin "to collect from colleagues in other disciplines enough information about what they do in their courses to make it possible to determine where and how [information and resource technology] might be integrated into what is already going on."[19]

Hatch concluded her speech with a description of a writing course linked to an "Introduction to Ancient Art History" course that successfully integrated research skills into the curriculum. Key to the success of this collaboration is having the librarian, who earlier introduced students to research tools and resources targeted to the specific topic, available to dialogue with students regarding what they encountered in their initial research efforts. Students submit their questions in advance of the session so that the librarian can answer their specific questions and follow up on related issues. Hatch reported that "many students rank this interaction with the librarian as one of the most valuable aspects of her writing course."[20]

Steve McKinzie, a librarian at Dickinson College in Carlisle, Pennsylvania, concurs with Hatch. He believes that research, like writing, "merits a more thorough and comprehensive commitment. . . . Colleges and universities have to replace their present well-intentioned approach to research instruction with a sustained, comprehensive vision—one that teaches research skills in a variety of classes and contexts."[21]

PLANNING FOR GENERAL EDUCATION

The best place to start information literacy planning is with general education or core curriculum, where concerns for competencies that all students should acquire provide a natural home for the discussions of information literacy abilities. Described below are some functioning models—at various stages of development—that are part of an ever growing body of currently in-place information literacy programs.

These multifaceted information literacy programs provide good models for consideration by other campuses seeking to develop a curriculum design for integrating information literacy across the curriculum.

Northwest Missouri State University

Northwest Missouri State has taken a tiered approach to its instructional efforts which, with its Olympic flavor, targets increasingly sophisticated skills as they are needed. The components of the program, called "MEDAL" (Making Education Available in the Library), are displayed in Figure 3-1.

The MEDAL program is both formally and informally assessed on an ongoing basis, and evaluations have revealed that "faculty are pleased with the types of sources retrieved and their impact on student work."[22]

California State University, San Marcos

California State University, San Marcos (CSUSM), the newest public university built in California, boasts an undergraduate campus commitment to information literacy. The school's focus on information literacy has resulted in a view of the library as a "learning laboratory" and in the integration of information literacy learning opportunities throughout the general education

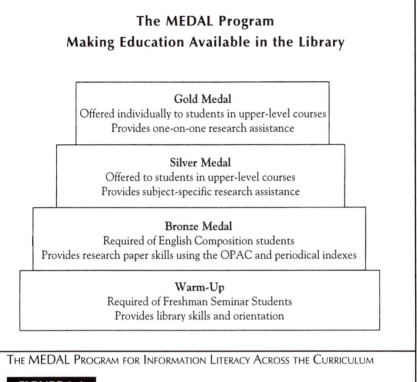

The MEDAL Program
Making Education Available in the Library

Gold Medal
Offered individually to students in upper-level courses
Provides one-on-one research assistance

Silver Medal
Offered to students in upper-level courses
Provides subject-specific research assistance

Bronze Medal
Required of English Composition students
Provides research paper skills using the OPAC and periodical indexes

Warm-Up
Required of Freshman Seminar Students
Provides library skills and orientation

THE MEDAL PROGRAM FOR INFORMATION LITERACY ACROSS THE CURRICULUM

FIGURE 3-1

program. For instance, the 48-hour general education program is divided into five categories: basic skills, math and science, humanities and arts, social sciences, and lifelong understanding. Each area has separate goals, objectives, and competency statements. In the basic skills area, students learn "how to use a library . . . and the courses include aspects of evaluation of sources, critical thinking and critical listening."[23]

Within the three core subject areas, the criteria for lower-division general education courses require that the faculty demonstrate how they will incorporate information literacy skills and library use into their courses. To ensure that these plans will be realized, a librarian—as part of all the instructional teams—is assigned to each of the core courses in the sciences, humanities, and social sciences.

> Librarians teach students how researchers in the various disciplines work. They introduce students to basic information resources in those disciplines and help them develop the skills necessary to use them. For example, the first goal of the ACRL Model Statement of Objectives, "How information is identified and defined by experts, becomes the goal in Area B (math and science)."[24]

Towson University

One of the best comprehensive planning processes to integrate information resources and technology into the curriculum is at Towson University (TU) in Maryland. In the early 1990s, a faculty committee, whose purpose was to determine if the existing general education requirements were adequate, concluded that four major areas needed to be addressed. Among them was the startling realization that although the school had a long commitment to a liberal arts philosophy—including preparing students for lifelong learning—many students were reaching their senior year with only elementary research capabilities. In conjunction with this finding, the same faculty inquiry determined that traditional research skills were no longer adequate. Students needed to acquire research techniques that have been made possible by newer information technologies. The committee was most concerned about the need for students to be able evaluators of the relative quality of varying information resources.

As these deliberations were under way, Jim Clements and Liz Manguarian, TU faculty members in computer science, with the support of Dean Larry Boucher, involved themselves in curriculum discussions within the College of Natural and Mathematical Sciences (CONAMS). These discussions grew out of a retreat where TU academics and students met with science and technology employers to evaluate the quality of TU graduates. The findings were alarming. The business leaders reported that "their new employees could do chemistry, math, and biology. But Towson had not provided their companies with people who could work in teams, who could communicate effectively, and who could think critically."[25]

When CONAMS personnel set out to create a course that would address these insufficiencies, they inadvertently developed a model that could be used campuswide to address information literacy needs. Entitled "The Transition Course," it was first offered on a volunteer basis to freshmen in the fall of 1994. The goals of the new course were to produce graduates who could

- communicate effectively
- work successfully in teams
- solve problems
- think creatively
- use information technology

The course was successful, and by the fall of 1996, four additional three-credit courses were added just to meet the "Using Information" general education requirement; a year later that number increased to 10.

Figure 3-2 displays the course descriptions and student learning objectives for the two three-credit courses that evolved directly from the retreat.[26]

Towson Transition Course: Using Information Effectively in Science

Course Description:
Introduction to information processing, problem solving techniques, creative thinking skills, communication skills, team building, and professional ethics in a scientific environment. Emphasis will be placed on the use of information technology to retrieve, filter, process, and evaluate data and information. This course is intended for freshman CONAMS students. Five contact hours. (3 credits)

The Student Will:
1) explore how technology can be used to retrieve, process, and communicate information
2) understand methods and models of investigation in science and mathematics
3) practice and improve the use of communication skills
4) understand the importance of team building and team work
5) learn the fundamentals of problem solving and critical thinking
6) learn the importance of creative thinking in science
7) learn to appreciate the need for ethics in a scientific environment

Information & Technology for Business

Course Description:
Introduction to the use of information technology to retrieve, filter, process, classify, sort, and evaluate data and information in a business environment. Problem solving, creative thinking, effective communication, team building, and professional ethics within an information systems framework. Labs covering library information systems, the Internet, word processing, presentation software, spreadsheets, and databases will be emphasized in the course.

The Student Will:
1) explore how technology can be used to store, retrieve, filter, classify, sort, process, evaluate, and communicate information effectively
2) learn how to use library information systems, the Internet, word processing, presentation software, spreadsheets, and database software to assist with the effective use of information
3) learn the fundamentals of problem solving and critical thinking as applied to information systems
4) learn the importance of the creative use of information in business
5) learn to appreciate the need for ethics when using information and technology

TRANSITION COURSE: DESCRIPTIONS AND OBJECTIVES

FIGURE 3-2

Figure 3-3 provides brief descriptions of three other general education courses that evolved from the initial transition course to provide a flavor of how the course varies to suit different disciplines.[27]

INSTRUCTIONAL TECHNOLOGY 201
Using Information Effectively in Education

An introduction to gathering, evaluating, and communicating information. Emphasis will be on using team collaboration and problem solving to examine current issues in education.

INTERDISCIPLINARY LIBERAL ARTS 101
Using Information in the Social Sciences

Obtaining, evaluating, and presenting social science information, emphasizing the scientific method, critical thinking using logical and statistical analysis, and problems of inference. Attention to practical search and analysis skills, using computerized databases, Internet applications, statistical software, and effective communication. Recommended for social science students.

PHILOSOPHY 102
Using Information Effectively in Philosophy

Introduction to information gathering, evaluation, and communication in philosophy. The course seeks to develop critical thinking and problem solving techniques, communication and team building skills in the context of grappling with age-old problems in philosophy. Emphasis will be placed on the use of information technology to retrieve and on the use of traditional philosophical techniques of argument analysis and evaluations. Intended for freshman students.

THEATRE ARTS 125
Script Analysis

Study of the play, emphasizing the analysis of structure, genre, theme, style, character, language, dramatic event, and point of view of actor, director, designer, critic, and audience. Introduction to theatre research methods.

OTHER GENERAL EDUCATION COURSES THAT EVOLVED FROM THE TRANSITION COURSE

FIGURE 3-3

The TU model is an exceptional information literacy program that is well worth emulating for a number of reasons. First, both faculty and employers initially identified the need for students to improve their research, problem-solving, and critical-thinking skills. The courses were also developed with a firm understanding of their importance to student success—both in school and beyond school.

Second, the course offering the foundation for information literacy is a part of the students' general education requirements, and is only one of a series of courses tailored to the different needs of the various disciplines. (The differences between the two courses within the College of Natural and Mathematical Sciences is particularly worth noting.)

Third, the effectiveness of any three-credit required general education course on information literacy can be significantly enhanced if faculty can think of creative ways to individualize the learning outcomes and the course syllabi to their own individual disciplines. During any such planning, faculty should focus on what is most appropriately covered in the general education courses versus what is best left to be integrated and built upon throughout the curriculum of their various academic programs.

Fourth, planning for information literacy across the curriculum would benefit from following TU's example by starting out with a clear idea of what the end result of the program should be in terms of student learning. Then those goals should appear in university and departmental publications. Indeed, properly packaged, such statements can be useful recruitment tools because both students and parents are aware of national and state concerns for the Information Highway—such as the crash of America Online—and the difficulty of finding information needed in daily life.

Purdue University

Librarians at Purdue University have developed one of the best sets of learning outcome statements in use today. As a result of a priority in their strategic plan to "Redefine User Instruction," the Purdue librarians have moved away from single lectures and open workshops to collaboration with faculty in the development of an information literacy curriculum that is integrated throughout the university curriculum.

As a part of their planning process, the librarians have identified the following six goals for all students to achieve during their undergraduate years:

- User understands the role, value, and power of information in modern society.
- User understands and is able to communicate his/her specific needs for information.
- User understands that information varies in its organization, content, and format.
- User can retrieve information from a variety of systems and in various formats.
- User can evaluate information sources.
- User understands how to organize information effectively.[28]

In addition to such goal statements, many campuses have also developed a longer statement that indicates how the overall goals break down into learning objectives—particularly as they relate to the general education portion of student learning. Such statements provide a valuable checklist for curriculum planners to ensure that they have covered all their bases. In the same vein, the Association of College & Research Libraries has developed a "Model Statement of Objectives for Academic Bibliographic Instruction" as a useful checklist for developing such objectives. However, Purdue took this concept one step further when it supported each goal with specific learning objectives and tied each of the following three levels of mastery with each objective:

> Level I: orientation which is primarily designed as an interactive, learner-centered, self-paced tutorial to be used by beginning students

> Level II: developing mental models for finding, evaluating and using information

> Level III: learning to apply the information strategy models to a discipline[29]

Although the librarians at Purdue are independently offering Level I components, they are now also in the process of marketing their library-user instruction program for Levels II and III to classroom faculty.

Beyond the general education level, each degree program should also have a statement of learning outcomes that is appropriate to the literature and information of its field. National professional and discipline organizations should adopt statements of learning outcomes that can serve as a basis for campus information literacy efforts. Employers, meanwhile, are already calling for problem solving and other desirable on-the-job skills.

North Dakota State University

In an effort to identify what types of information management skills are needed in the workplace today, North Dakota State University (NDSU) invited local employers of their graduates in the areas of business and engineering to meet on campus with faculty and librarians to describe their current information needs. The results of that meeting became the basis for the development of class assignments in which students develop information management abilities that would clearly be useful on the job.[30] This approach to planning information literacy programs heightens the ultimate learning experience because faculty and students alike know that the information management process students are learning in the academic setting is the same process they will use in the workplace. This approach to identifying what types of information management skills students will need after graduation seems a meaningful project for a college's advisory board. Unfortunately, a change in campus administration at NDSU brought this project to a standstill.

The University of Washington

Perhaps the best place to end this section is with the UWired Project at the University of Washington (UW) because the project illustrates how information literacy can impact the very fiber of the whole educational process.* By the way it integrates information resources and technology into the curriculum, UWired projects a view of the future. Begun in 1994 under the direction of Louis Fox in the Office of Undergraduate Education, the program today is well integrated across the curriculum thanks to the hard work of many people and the support of Richard McCormick, the University of Washington's new president.

Below is a brief description of the intent of the UWired Project.

> In response to the challenges of bringing technology into the service of teaching and learning, the new information literacy, and the creation of community at a large university, the University of Washington developed a holistic, campus-wide approach called UWired. The primary goal of UWired is to create an electronic community in which communication and information technologies become integral to teaching and learning.
>
> UWired addresses faculty development, active student learning, and facilities redesign. UWired brings together diverse expertise and support to enhance campus-wide learning and teaching. UWired seeks to go beyond technology—offering sustained discipline-specific instruction, useful educational applications of technology, faculty and librarian development, and requisite facilities and infrastructure. . . .[31]

The program was designed to support the institutional goals of the university, which are to emphasize "the mastery of methods of inquiry and [to] foster those qualities of mind that encourage mature and independent judgement."[32] UWired was also designed to accomplish the following learning goals:

- integrates electronic communication and information literacy skills into teaching and learning
- creates learning communities not bound by place or time
- encourages intellectual engagement among faculty, librarians, and students
- integrates appropriate technology into curriculum content and delivery
- explores models for institutional collaboration

---

*A similar undertaking exists at the University of Iowa, where the Information Arcade is collaboratively administered by the University Libraries and the Office of Information Technology. The Information Arcade is designed "to support the use of electronic resources in research, teaching, and independent learning." For more information on this program, see Anita K. Lowry, "The Information Arcade at the University of Iowa," *Cause/Effect*, 17 (Fall, 1994), 38-44.

In 1995, UW faculty members across the curriculum were solicited to develop courses that integrated information resources and technology with teaching and learning. To date, 13 courses, including Czech literature, environmental statistics, economic geography, journalism, and radiology, have been updated to include technology and networked information. Faculty members who teach these courses benefit from extra technical support, specialized software, and a librarian teaching partner. More detailed information about this extraordinary program is available at http://www.washington.edu/uwired/. In addition, Betsy Wilson, associate director of Libraries for Public Services, will publish two major articles about UWired in 1997.[33]

ASSESSMENT ISSUES

Because assessment is a vital part of any learning enterprise, standard assessment tools, such as class grades, accreditation, and promotions and tenure, have been around for a long time. However, starting with the reform reports of the 1980s, serious questions about the quality and significance of academic assessment have been raised and have led to the development of new assessment tools, such as teaching portfolios and capstone courses. It is within this new, richer context of assessment tools that the following discussion about information literacy programs must be set. In addition, this discussion considers assessment at three specific levels: student project/assignment evaluation, student learning outcomes assessment, and departmental and campus assessments.

Student Project/Assignment Evaluation

This level of assessment provides the basic building blocks that motivate students to acquire information literacy abilities. Students value what faculty value, and what is evaluated—what is graded by faculty—is what students perceive as being important. Thus, it is not enough for faculty simply to send students off to library workshops with an inspiring speech that equates good research with academic success and lifelong learning. Experience shows that students will not give much credibility to any such assignment unless the course syllabus clearly states that their research efforts will be assessed, and that those evaluations will constitute a significant proportion of their course grade. The more professors place importance on research and other information literacy skills, the more the students will also. The principle is the same in regard to graded versus pass/fail courses; whatever is most important is graded and whatever is graded with the most weight is considered the most important aspect of the course by students.

Thus, whenever assessment of student performance occurs, information literacy abilities should be included. If students are required to take a capstone course, the assessment criteria for that course should include how they are able to identify, locate, evaluate, and effectively use information. The use of student portfolios should include provisions that measure growth in information management skills as well as content areas. Moreover, to help facilitate such inclusion, faculty members could greatly benefit from tip sheets on effective ways of evaluating students' research abilities within course assignments.

Student Learning Outcomes Assessment

Not all campuses are seriously engaged in evaluating what students have learned or gained from their college educations. However, where such efforts are in place or being developed, information literacy abilities should be incorporated into the assessment program. The final question in the 1990 "Framework for Outcomes Assessment" issued by the Commission on Higher Education (CHE) of the Middle States Association of Colleges and Schools goes to the heart of the value-added question when it asks, ". . . are students required to use increasingly complex library research skills?"[34]   This question implies a need for both a planned effort on the part of the institution, as well as documented progress on the part of students. Moreover, because lifelong learning is a highly desirable learning outcome for all students, students should begin developing this habit in the campus library.

Departmental and Campus Assessments

Ultimately, what makes the greatest impact on students is the collective assessment efforts within a particular school or college—plus what is assessed within the general education requirements that constitute the campuswide assessment. As a result, an across-the-curriculum strategy is needed for ensuring that all students, regardless of their major fields of study, receive a sequential and adequate set of learning opportunities that will allow them to develop both general and subject-specific information management skills. For example, at King's College in Wilkes-Barre, Pennsylvania, the comprehensive assessment program includes the following eight transferable skills of liberal learning:

- critical thinking
- effective writing
- effective oral communication
- library and information literacy
- computer competency
- quantitative reasoning
- creative thinking and problem solving
- moral reasoning[35]

All departments and programs are required to show how each of the above skills applies within the context of the major. Then department members must divide the skills into specific competencies for students to develop throughout their undergraduate years in both core and major courses.

For majors in the Marketing Department at King's College, the library and information literacy competency is as follows:

> The student majoring in Marketing will be able to plan and implement
> comprehensive search strategies, to use sophisticated forms of library
> and information technology, and to employ research techniques ap-
> propriate to marketing research and the subsequent development of
> marketing plans.[36]

From this competency statement, a competency growth plan that encom-passes what should be learned across the marketing curriculum has been developed. The plan is a good example of how information literacy goals can be integrated into a subject-specific curriculum. (The competency growth plan in library and information literacy for students majoring in marketing at Kings College is reprinted in its entirety in Appendix E).

A good, more generic starting point for planning assessment of departmental or campus information literacy programs is the following set of questions in the 1990 CHE framework statement:

- How many syllabi include library-based assignments?
- What is the nature of those assignments?
- Are they appropriate for the program and its students?
- Do they show evidence of thought and creativity?
- Do they promote active learning?
- Do they take advantage of primary sources when appropriate?
- Do they display a knowledge of the range of resources available to students at the institution?
- Is there a sense that, as students progress from the beginning of the degree program to its conclusion, they are required to use increasingly complex library research skills?[37]

Careful efforts to coordinate assessment of information literacy perfor-mance across the curriculum will help create a positive climate for goal-directed learning on any campus.

CONCLUSION

Common sense and experience tell us most of what we know about what works and what does not work in information literacy programs. Once faculty accept the importance of information literacy to ensure the academic and career success of their students, and once they seriously plan for and assess achievement of that goal, then students will graduate as lifelong learners and productive citizens for an Information Age.

NOTES

1. Patricia Daragan and Gwendolyn Stevens, "Developing Lifelong Learners: An Investigative and Developmental Approach to Information Literacy," *Research Strategies*, 14 (Spring 1996), p. 68-81.
2. Harlan Cleveland, *The Knowledge Executive: Leadership in an Information Society* (New York: Truman Tally Books/E.P. Dutton, 1985), 28-33.
3. "Librarians and Faculty Members: Model Partnerships for Improving Undergraduate Instruction," *Washington Center News*, 5 (Winter 1991), 13.
4. Betsy Porter, John A. Lanning, and Beth Forrest Warner, "Team Teaching the Chemical Literature," in *Preparing for the 21st Century: Proceedings of the Mountain Plains Library Association*, edited by Sue Hatfield (Emporia, KS: Emporia State University Press, 1986), 55-61.
5. Patricia Senn Breivik, "UGE 100: Information Power Course Redesign," proposal for Wayne State University collaboration with The Lake Group, Inc., December 2, 1996, 10-11.
6. Major Owens, "State Government and Libraries," *Library Journal*, 101 (January 1, 1976), 27.
7. Patrick Hill, "Who Will Lead the Reform of Higher Education? Librarians, Of Course!" *Washington Center News*, 5 (Winter 1991), 8.
8. Janet Owens and Kathryn Kaya, syllabus for Information Literacy Course-LIBR121 at Montana State University, September 11, 1995.
9. Judy Reynolds, California State University, e-mail to the author, December 13, 1996.
10. Ibid.
11. Michael Buckland, "The 'Liberal Arts' of Library and Information Science and the Research University Environment," a paper presented at the Second International Conference on Conceptions of Library and Information Science: Integration in Perspective, Copenhagen, Denmark, October 13-14, 1995, 4.
12. Ibid., 14.
13. Barbara MacAdam, letter to Jeanine Taylor, Wayne State University, January 24, 1997.
14. Barbara MacAdam, syllabus for Knowledge and Society in the Information Age, Honors 251 at the University of Michigan, January 1997.
15. Taken from information submitted by Shelton State Community College in response to a 1994/1995 survey regarding information literacy programs conducted by the Commission on Higher Education of the Middle States Association of Colleges and Schools, the Western Association of Schools and Colleges, and the Association of College and Research Libraries.
16. Kelley Emmons McHenry, J. T. Stewart, and Jennifer L. Wu, "Teaching Resource-Based Learning and Diversity," *Information Literacy: Developing Students as Independent Learners*, edited by D. W. Farmer and Terrence F. Mech, no. 78 (San Francisco: Jossey-Bass Publishers, Summer 1992), 57.
17. Ibid., 57-58.
18. "Linked Courses: A Method to Reinforce Basic Skills," *Electric Library*, Weber State University, Ogden, UT, Internet, March 13, 1997.

19. Deborah Hatch, "Integrating Library Instruction Across the Curriculum: Some Lessons from Writing Across the Curriculum Programs," *Washington Center News*, 5 (Winter 1991), 9-11.

20. Ibid., 11.

21. Steve McKinzie, "Research Across the Curriculum," *C&RL News*, No. 6 (June 1995), 417.

22. Connie Ury, "A Tiered Approach to Bibliographic Instruction: The MEDAL Program," *Research Strategies*, 10 (Fall 1994), 250.

23. Gabriela Sonntag and Donna M. Ohr, "The Development of a Lower-Division, General Education, Course-Integrated Information Literacy Program," *College & Research Libraries*, 57 (July, 1996), 335.

24. Ibid.

25. Mike Bowler, "An Experiment in Thinking," *The Sun: Education* (December 10, 1995), 1,4.

26. Taken from curriculum material supplied by Dr. James Clement, College of Material and Materialized Sciences, Towson University, Towson, MD, 1997.

27. Towson University Undergraduate Course Listings, Towson, MD, 1996, 69, 105, 139.

28. Taken from information submitted by Purdue University in response to a 1994/1995 survey regarding information literacy programs conducted by the Commission on Higher Education of the Middle States Association of Colleges and Schools, the Western Association of Schools and Colleges, and the Association of College and Research Libraries.

29. Ibid.

30. Faculty administrators interviewed by author on April 27, 1995, at North Dakota State University in Fargo, ND.

31. Betsy Wilson, "U-Wired: Enhancing, Teaching, Learning, and Technology through Collaboration," *Collaboration and Instructional Design in a Virtual Environment* (Foundations of Library and Information Science Series) (Greenwich, CT: JAI Press, 1997), 1.

32. Ibid.

33. Ibid.

34. The Commission on Higher Education of the Middle States Association of Colleges and Schools, *Frameworks for Outcomes Assessment* (Philadelphia: Visual Arts Press, 1990), 18.

35. Cheryl O'Hara, "The Assessment Program at Kings College," King's College, Wilkes-Barre, PA, February 10, 1997 [photocopy].

36. "Competency Growth Plan in Library and Information Literacy for Students Majoring in Marketing," unpublished guidelines sent to author from King's College, Wilkes-Barre, PA, February 13, 1997 [photocopy].

37. The Commission on Higher Education, *Frameworks*, 18.

CHAPTER 4

Discipline-Specific Models

Information can be and is often used as a power to influence, to persuade, to attempt to control outcomes, to generate public opinion, to influence elections and decisions. As power, information is a basic tool or key to competing successfully.

—Nolan Bowie

Planning for information literacy across the curriculum must include the tailoring of learning experiences to the literature of the various disciplines and fields of study and to eventual on-the-job information management needs. Given the importance of these learning opportunities to fostering the type of workers that employers demand from higher education, local and statewide business leaders and employers must be involved in determining what information competencies should be mastered across the curriculum. This chapter highlights a series of discipline-specific examples of resource-based learning programs that are already functioning on campuses across the United States.

However, not all the following examples are set within the context of a well-thought-out information literacy program. Some are fairly isolated efforts that exist only because of the insights and commitments of individual faculty and librarians. However, having a serious, widespread, and ongoing impact on students' learning will require that discipline-specific efforts be coordinated with other efforts within the department's programs so that they collectively and systematically build upon the foundation of more generic information literacy abilities mastered within the general education or core curriculum.

All the following examples will certainly stimulate ideas for approaches that academic departments could explore as they establish their information literacy programs. Moreover, there is definitely some commonality within the information seeking and evaluation process that can be transferred from one body of knowledge to another. As a result, insights may be gained from examples even outside one's own discipline.

Given the popularity of such examples or models, the ERIC Clearinghouse on Information Resources established a World Wide Web site in 1997 to encourage the showcasing of in-practice models of information literacy. Academicians wishing to post or read such information can access the site at http://ericir.syr.edu/nfil.

A SUBJECT-SPECIFIC APPROACH*

One of the most carefully constructed approaches to developing an information literacy curriculum within a professional curriculum from an education perspective was devised during the 1995/96 school year at Wayne State University in Detroit by Dr. Bruce D. Friedman of the School of Social Work and by Dane Ward, the librarian liaison to the school. Friedman and Ward received a competitive grant from the university for integrating information resources and technology into the curriculum. They considered such an integration essential because, despite the "explosion of information available in social work topics" during the previous 20 years, there was a perceived "inability of social workers to remain current" in their field. This situation was "compounded by the demands being placed on the field by collateral systems such as managed care and the insurance companies." Friedman and Ward also reasoned that such integration was essential for the following reasons:

> Student interest in achieving the knowledge and skills to successfully utilize information resources and technology is directly related to the information technology skills used to succeed while in Social Work programs. The more faculty require students to acquire technology skills the greater skills students will develop. However, it is rare for a student to seek and acquire technology skills on her/his own. This is partially because the student has so much work that has to be done there is little time to reflect or venture out on her/his own. Unless the student can see the relationship to acquiring the skill, then there is little likelihood that the student will seek to learn the skill.[1]

Friedman, Ward, and Art Biagianti, another colleague from the library at the Mandel School of Applied Social Sciences in Cleveland, Ohio, strongly believe that the abilities of students and practitioners "to navigate the chang-

---

*Because the following examples were selected to provide a good sampling of approaches currently being taken to integrate information resources and technology into the curriculum, matters of geographical or institutional distribution were not considered. A secondary objective was to provide a reasonably broad sampling of disciplines. Also, because existing literature served as the basis for the examples in this chapter, several examples appear for some disciplines while other disciplines are not represented at all. Enough information is provided for each example to allow the reader to obtain additional information if desired.

ing information environment will depend on their competence in thinking critically about information, information resources, and the new technologies."[2] All three men believe critical thinking skills are the key. Using Benjamin Bloom's *Taxonomy of Educational Objectives* as a tool for benchmarking their instructional efforts, they projected how a course might be constructed.

By comparing class assignments and discussion questions with Bloom's *Taxonomy*, faculty may determine with fair accuracy the levels of cognitive challenge presented to their students. The following examples illustrate the relationship between Bloom's levels and various questions and assignments:

> During one class, the instructor asks students to name the electronic index that contains journal research in Social Work. They recall information (Level 1) from a previous lecture or hands-on experience. Later, they are asked to explain the difference between the electronic catalog and the electronic indexes in terms of their contents. This question requires students to **comprehend** (Level 2) differences between resources citing books and articles.

> After some brief instruction on the operating principles of an electronic index, students receive an assignment requiring them to find articles on genograms. They must understand concepts as well as how to **apply what they've learned** (Level 3). As a follow-up assignment, students search for articles about "crisis intervention" using "subject" and "keyword" strategies (with such Boolean operators as "and," "or," "not," and "adj"). They then **analyze** the results (Level 4) to learn what each search retrieved and why.

> Later in the semester, after students have mastered various functions in this database, they are asked to experiment with an entirely different type of information retrieval system. Given a list of features to find and explore, students study this new database, pull together or synthesize (Level 5) their new understanding to complete further searches on their given topic of "crisis intervention." Finally, students compare and **evaluate** (Level 6) the two databases to determine the effectiveness of each system in finding research on Social Work topics.[3]

Although few faculty/librarian teams are likely to be so systematic about their development of resource-based learning initiatives, such an approach can certainly do much to take the guesswork out of new offerings. This example also underscores the value of collaboration, which is a recurring theme in most of the examples that follow. Moreover, because serious planning and teamwork almost always result in a quality "product," the faculty members in the WSU College of Social Work are now working to integrate information literacy throughout the school's entire curriculum. Described below are other specific examples of information literacy in action on campuses across the United States.

AGRICULTURE/ECONOMICS

One of the earliest information literacy initiatives to be based in research and to holistically address a targeted subject area was developed in 1986 by Jan Kennedy Olsen and Bill Coons, librarians at Cornell University's Mann Library. The Department of Agricultural Economics agreed to work with the Mann Library faculty to develop a core program that used resource-based courses. They jointly created a series of goals and objectives that applied to a sequence of classes from the sophomore to the senior year.

"Information Resources for Business Decision Making," a resource-based course within the agricultural economics curriculum, is just one result of this collaboration. After students are familiar with the external business databases, they are assigned case studies that necessitate the use of these databases. Then they must analyze the information obtained from the databases to complete the assignment. For example, the assigned case study called "Site Selection" requires students to imagine they are the vice president of facilities planning for a firm that is planning a move to upstate New York. The vice president's job is to analyze all available data on three potential sites and make a recommendation. This assignment requires that students retrieve data on the three sites, make a table of their reported values, and interpret those findings.[4]

BUSINESS

An article in the Spring 1996 *Sloan Management Review* presents some serious challenges to the way many schools of business seem to ignore changes in the workplace brought on by the Information Age.

> The international data highway will transform business education, although not necessarily its traditional supplier, the business school. Will the business school remain insulated from the knowledge revolution? Will it play a leadership role? Will it wither away?[5]

A summary of the lack of information literacy efforts within schools of business by the American Association of Collegiate Schools of Business is well documented in the September/October 1994 issue of the *Journal of Education for Business* by Douglass K. Hawes, then a faculty member at the University of Wyoming. He reports that the literature review of what is being done in business schools provides a few good practicing models of how information literacy efforts have been integrated into the curriculum, including stand-alone courses, inclusion in capstone courses, and required self-teaching exercises. Nevertheless, Hawes concludes that "today's business school graduate is not being adequately prepared to function in an information literate fashion in a world of knowledge workers."[6]

The need for improvement in the preparation of business leaders has also been underscored by Peter Drucker, the internationally respected consultant and professor of management. In the December 1, 1992, issue of the *Wall Street Journal*,[7] he stated the following:

> Executives have become computer-literate. The younger ones, especially, know more about the way the computer works than they know about the mechanics of the automobile or the telephone. But not many executives are information literate. They know how to get data, but most still have to learn how to use data. . . . Few executives yet know how to ask: "What information do I need to do my job? When do I need it? In what form? And from whom should I be getting it?" Fewer still ask: "What new tasks can I tackle now that I get all these data? Which old tasks should I abandon? Which tasks should I do differently?" . . . A "database," no matter how copious, is not information. It is information's ore. For raw material to become information, it must be organized for a task, directed toward specific performance, applied to a decision. Raw material cannot do that itself.

Drucker concluded by saying that this knowledge society "requires that its members learn how to learn."

Marketing

Realizing that strong marketing skills are based on accurate information gathering for product planning, pricing, promotion, and distribution, Vaughan C. Judd, head of the marketing department, and Betty J. Tims, coordinator of government information and bibliographic instruction, at the library at Auburn University at Montgomery in Montgomery, Alabama, developed four workshops. Targeted at four different marketing courses, the workshops clearly showed how to integrate research and retrieval skills with course instruction. The workshops, taught by an instructor and librarian team, modelled how marketing strategies can be applied to secondary data that can be gathered mostly from government documents.

From provided data sources, students research realistic scenarios for each case study. The instructor and librarian then interactively discuss the assigned scenarios and the various resources available for research and analysis. Specifically, they show students how to find, read, and interpret the relevant government data appropriate to each scenario.[8]

Business Policy

The University of Maryland Eastern Shore's Department of Business and Economics has developed a course for business administration majors that allows students to master skills necessary for making and implementing decisions that are often critical to an organization's future. Using actual management decision-making situations, students must verbally convince their fellow students of the validity of their analysis of each of their cases.

In formulating their analysis, students are required to use outside business resources, such as the *Wall Street Journal* and *Business Week*. Library research skills are explored during the second week of class, and these skills are not only needed for the case studies but are critical for a later assignment that requires students to prepare an extensive report on a corporation by analyzing all available materials. These reports are then presented orally to the class.[9]

COMMUNICATIONS AND FINE AND PERFORMING ARTS

Fundamental to all communications courses is the belief that communication in mass media is dependent on the ability of a writer or speaker to "analyze and synthesize information effectively."[10] Thus, anyone being trained in any of the areas of communication must be able to acquire needed information, evaluate it critically, and use it professionally.

Communication

One example of resource-based learning within the communications discipline is modeled on a course that originated at the University of Minnesota and was later adapted by the University of Michigan. Committed to information literacy, Barbara MacAdam and the communications faculty at the University of Michigan developed an information-gathering course for mass media that is a prerequisite for all writing classes in communication. In addition, all faculty members are encouraged to illustrate and emphasize through their regular assignments the vast amount of information sources available. Student assignments are also geared to apply information-gathering techniques to potentially real situations to reinforce learned skills. By practicing the resource-based learning skills in class, students have the wonderful opportunity to see for themselves how important these skills are to them academically and personally.[11] Although the library is used as a starting point, the students are encouraged to explore other areas of relevant material, such as personal interviews and observations.

Theater

Now retired, Dr. Richard Knaub, professor of theater and dance at the University of Colorado in Boulder, was an early proponent of information literacy. For many years he taught the research methods class in collaboration with librarians because he believed that research skills are necessary even in an area like theater—especially when working with nonprint (i.e., audiovisual) material. One of the ways Knaub's students practiced research skills was by preparing slide tape shows. Knaub often told the story of how this tradition first began.

> [A] graduate student who had done exhaustive research about women in the 19th Century American theatre . . . had found marvelous etchings and engravings and, later, some photos. It seemed a shame for such material to disappear into the stacks once more. In cooperation with the audio-visual librarian, Dinah prepared a tape lecture illustrated by slides which the library made from the illustrations she had found.[12]

ENGINEERING

When the graduate engineering chair at Wayne State University raised concerns about the inability of many of the graduate students in his department to do effective research, the engineering librarian, H. Stephen McMinn, identified a series of desirable skills outcomes and proposed three possible levels at which those skills could be achieved. The highlights of that proposal, entitled *Proposal to the College of Engineering for the Development of Student Research Skills,* are outlined below:

Identification of Skills

There are a number of information literacy skills that could be identified as being important to *all students*, including those in the College of Engineering, to facilitate lifelong learning. A sampling of these skills are as follows.

1. Basic Skills
    Identifying and defining the information need
    Locating information—Using the online catalog
    Information needs/utilization of different disciplines
2. Information Gathering Skills
    Primary vs. secondary sources
    Types of primary information sources
    Types of secondary information sources
    Evaluating indexes and abstracts
3. Computerized Database Searching
    Basics of searching—Boolean operators
    Search engines
    Modifying searches
    Thesauri and user aids
4. Citing Information
    Standard formats
    Abbreviations
    Relevancy
5. Tricks of the Trade
    Using citation analysis
    Using informal networks

---

6. Evaluation of Sources
   Reviews
   Professional reputation—Authors and Publishers
   Citation analysis

Delivery Options

1. Create a one-credit-hour course required for graduate students (optional for undergraduates) devoted solely to students acquiring research skills that will be needed for successful completion of the course and research assignments.
2. Develop an across-the-curriculum approach by determining appropriate places within the current curriculum, such as within design or writing intensive courses, where the learning of needed information literacy skills could best be incorporated.
3. Create a three-credit-hour course that encompasses all the skills above plus the lifelong learning skills important to engineering students as expressed by employers at the Ford/WSU Continuous Quality Improvement (CQI) Symposium.[13]

Introduction to Engineering

While the above proposal is still in the planning stage at Wayne State, Rensselaer Polytechnic Institute's School of Engineering has already incorporated resource-based learning into the engineering curriculum via the engineering design courses. "Introduction to Engineering" (IED) is a required course for the approximately 3,700 second-year engineering majors. The course, which is taught collaboratively by the engineering faculty and librarians, consists of a design problem created by the instructor.

During the course, students form teams to define a problem quantitatively and qualitatively, to generate and evaluate concepts, and to select a design concept to pursue. At the end of the semester, the teams present to the class detailed manufacturing and assembly plans for a working prototype, an actual prototype, a proof-of-principle, and a test for customer satisfaction. While the students work in groups, the engineering instructor and librarian circulate, serving as facilitators by answering questions and providing direction as needed.

The engineering instructors have identified the following objectives for the IED course:

- To provide a successful design-build-test experience emphasizing the importance of high-quality, innovative, fast, and low-cost solutions.
- To present methods to systematically research, model, and analyze open-ended design problems, incorporating material from engineering science courses already taken.

- To provide an environment in which teamwork, group dynamics, and project management are not only important to the learning process, but are viewed as vital to success.
- To have students practice formal (documentation, presentations) and informal (design notebooks, memos, team discussions) oral and written technical communication.[14]

ENGLISH

English courses, especially those concerned with writing, are a natural place to emphasize research skills. What good is it for students to write well if they have nothing worth writing about? The grandest prose loses impact if filled with inaccuracies or vague, general statements. An excellent writer, therefore, must also be information literate to know where and how to get needed information, how to evaluate sources of information, and how to organize and analyze information. The following examples describe successful programs that produce information-literate writers.

Writing Across the Curriculum

The faculty and staff at Marygrove College in Detroit have conscientiously interwoven writing and information literacy programs across the curriculum; Marygrove students must take successive courses that build one upon the other. For example, English 102, the first-year seminar class, introduces information literacy and offers a basic understanding of the library along with instruction on available information technology. The next course, English 107, is a developmental writing course that integrates process-based research reading. English 108 is a required writing course that emphasizes process-based research, use of reference sources, source evaluation, and documentation.

At the junior and senior levels, Marygrove students are required to take English 312. This course covers more advanced written and oral communication and introduces discipline-specific research and specialized indexes. The capstone course is Senior Seminars 496, a required course that demonstrates students' information literacy skills in their major areas of study and concentrates on research procedures and projects.[15]

Expository Writing

After the members of the Faculty Council at Rutgers University's New Brunswick campus became convinced of the need for students to become information literate, they adopted a program for freshman English 102 that incorporates an information literacy component to ensure that all students will become information literate before graduation. Working cooperatively, the English faculty and librarians designed the course to incorporate hands-on experience, lecture, discussion, and written materials—all presented at junctures when students had specific information needs. During the fourth class meeting, librarians conduct a seminar to assist the students in conducting searches of journals and books related to their research topics. The seminar includes a discussion of print and CD-ROM indexes as well as searching strategies for online databases and catalogs. During the eighth week of class, English faculty and librarians meet with the students to discuss their research papers and resolve any problems they are having. The needs or weaknesses that most often surface include the range of periodical indexes, the quality of the reference sources, the bias in some literature, and the use of proper search terminology and strategies.

Using several assessment tools, the program facilitators received an overall positive assessment of the course, but found they needed to refine the course to make it as effective as possible.[16] One of the challenges pinpointed in the initial evaluations indicated that students wanted more demonstration of the computers and reference tools instead of the problem-solving seminar. Because all these skills are necessary learning components, modification of the course seems just a matter of fine tuning. To ensure that all students learn research skills, the English faculty and librarians are developing information literacy components for other writing courses that students may take instead of English 102.

Composition

The English faculty and librarians at Brigham Young University in Provo, Utah, have designed information literacy courses that include videotape presentations and the development of research strategies for specific topics that students select, research, and write about in a pro and con background study paper. This team-taught course was initially piloted in six English sections, but was eventually expanded to include all 95 sections of English composition.

In 1985, university administrators questioned the validity of librarians team teaching with regular faculty members; today, the team-teaching approach has expanded into various disciplines. In the mid-1980s, administrators believed that librarians should concentrate on collection development and library administration. Nevertheless, the library faculty eventually played a key role in the successful teaching of information literacy throughout the curriculum.

The university expanded its information literacy program to the junior and senior levels of instruction by developing course-related modules designed to meet specific objectives identified by faculty in various academic programs.

Initially, all subject librarians worked with any instructor who was interested, but demand often exceeded available staff time. As a partial response to this program, efforts were made to channel instruction into research methods courses.[17]

HUMANITIES

San Jose State University has developed a model, entitled Project Phoenix, that uses collaborative teaching and technological enhancements in humanities courses. The project has combined faculty with librarians—not only in teaching but also in curriculum development and assessment—because such a collaborative effort benefits the students by expanding their skills and hands-on experience. The selected humanities courses focus on changes in humanities resources, strategic searching, and critical thinking about the information gathered.

The Project Phoenix model includes lower- and upper-level humanities courses—ranging from the Summer Bridge Program, which teaches developmental skills for incoming freshman, to Art History 272, which is a graduate-level seminar on Renaissance Theory and Methodology. The courses include lectures, online sessions, peer group meetings, and research assignments. The major goal of Project Phoenix is to develop students into well-rounded citizens and lifelong learners.[18]

At Columbia University in New York City, a graduate-level humanities course has also been developed for students to master computer-based resources and methods of information retrieval relevant to the G4000 course. The students' main assignment during the course is to write a report on a subject of their choice. Initially, the students have to compile a selected bibliography of at least 20 references pertinent to their topic. They must use online, CD-ROM, and print resources to find their sources, and they must evaluate each research tool they use in their search process. In addition, students must analyze the various resources they use in their reports by discussing the strengths and weaknesses of each resource. This course always receives positive evaluations due to its "focus on disciplinary content, the individual research interests of the students, the demanding but practical research assignment, the in-class demonstrations of machine-readable resources, and the enthusiasm and expertise of the instructors."[19]

LAW

At the Neef Law Library at Wayne State University, "drop in" legal research sessions are offered during the day and evening. These sessions were developed as a supplement to the WSU Legal Research and Writing Program to provide directed instruction in legal research. Janice Seaberg, assistant director of the law library, developed the text used for the session. Entitled *Legal Research Sources: A Process Approach*, the text incorporates computer instruction, the Internet, and multimedia presentations. Seaberg is also currently working with LEXIS to put the text for the course on CD-ROM. Diana Pratt, the director of the WSU Legal Research and Writing Program, works with Seaberg to assess and refine the sessions each year.[20]

MEDICAL AND HEALTH-RELATED STUDIES

In any current discussion about almost any aspect of health care, the term *informatics* is bound to come up. *Health informatics* is an umbrella term that encompasses medicine, nursing, dental, and pharmacy informatics; a current working definition for health informatics is "the use of information technology (including both hardware and software) with information management concepts and methods to support the delivery of health care."[21]

Information literacy complements the concern for quality health care by empowering the patients and their families and friends to ask the right questions of health care providers; indeed, care personnel are beginning to emphasize their patients' need for information to make decisions.

> Only recently has the importance of the health care consumer been appreciated. The consumer shares an equal role, along with the provider, as a critical decision maker who drives the entire health care enterprise. We have entered into an era of healthcare informatics that empowers consumer decision making through the use of emerging interactive and multimedia technologies. These technologies can be distributed to virtually anyone, anywhere, at anytime. This new focus is the result of a paradigm change in the delivery of health care. Consumers want to actively participate and partner with healthcare providers and become an integral part of the decision-making process.[22]

Information literacy and informatics have several things in common: They are both concerned about meeting the practical information needs of people; to that end, they both seek to empower people to be effective information consumers.*

Community Heath Nursing

Because the primary goal of community health nursing programs is to study the promotion of health in communities, the faculty at the College of Nursing at

---

*For those particularly interested in informatics, a good body of literature exists on the topic, and further information is available through the small but active International Medical Informatic Association, 16, Place Longemalle, SH-1204 Geneva, Switzerland.

Rutgers, the State University of New Jersey, integrated informatics into their community health nursing program. The nursing faculty agreed that in addition to analyzing epidemiological data, community health nurses also needed to be able to create databases that could identify health trends. The nursing faculty at Rutgers also believed that graduates in this field needed other skills, such as the ability to write competitive grants, to manage information effectively, and to measure outcomes.

As a result, the curriculum developed for "Community Health Nursing Theory I" consists of a computer orientation workshop and a four-course sequence in "Community Health Theory and Practicum" that focuses on the assessment of patterns of a community's health. Both "Community Health Nursing Theory II" and "Community Health Nursing Practicum II" address acute and chronic alterations in health patterns of communities. Students in both courses are required to assess various community health databases and to collect data to answer various health issues within a community.

During the first year of the course on "Community Health Theory and Practicum," faculty and students discovered that existing databases are inadequate. Responding to that need, students developed the HP2000 Health Assessment Tool and Database, which was set up so that succeeding students could easily add more information. Since then, students have been able to successfully develop skills in data analysis and report generation.[23]

Community Nutrition

Montana State University in Bozeman integrates resource-based learning into several weeks of its junior-level community nutrition course. The objectives of the sessions are to introduce students to federal, state, and local government information and to make sure that students know how this information relates to their current and future needs. More specifically, the students learn the legislative process and what impact it has on community nutrition programs.

A campus librarian teaches two of the sessions. The first session reviews the legislative process and introduces sources that are helpful when researching government information. The second session demonstrates online search strategies, specifically ones that apply to the *Federal Register*. Students have usually given these sessions positive evaluations because they feel that the material covered in the sessions is relevant to their course work and helpful in completing their written assignments.[24]

Medicine

In 1994, the Medical College of Georgia began a pilot for a problem-based learning program, the goal of which is to empower future doctors to become self-directed learners. Faculty members coach small groups of students in their search for a solution to a fictitious clinical problem. As a group, students define the problem, analyze the facts, and formulate an hypothesis. Next, individual members of the group research a particular aspect of the problem. During the research aspect of this assignment, a faculty member and a librarian work together to assist the students in their retrieval of information and their MEDLINE search.

During subsequent classes, students present their findings to the class. Although students sometimes prove the accuracy of their hypotheses, many others have discovered that the researched data changes their view of the problem. When that happens, students present solutions that were not previously examined. Afterwards, the students summarize the cases and review and evaluate the processes they used to come to their conclusions.[25]

Gerontology

At the Institute of Gerontology at Wayne State University in Detroit, Professor Elizabeth A. Olson introduced an evidence-based practice approach to a course entitled "Seminar in Applied Research in Gerontology," which has been a required course since 1989. The ultimate objective for the course is to ensure a student's objective "consideration of the veracity of the findings of a given piece of research."[26]

In this course, which stresses the necessity of examining evidence in clinical decision making, students are not only expected to critique several research reports, but they must also present to the class their own research on aging that pertains to their own particular discipline. These presentations serve to demonstrate the students' understanding of research methods: what they are, why and when they are used, how to read them, and how to interpret what they mean.

Some of the techniques of evidence-based practice that are related to information literacy abilities are defining problems precisely, defining the information needed to solve the problems, conducting efficient searches of the literature, selecting the best of the relevant studies, and applying the rules of evidence to determine the validity of the studies. These techniques—along with skills in accessing and applying the findings of research reports and articles from a variety of fields—help students improve services to the elderly.

SCIENCES

Faculty at the University of Illinois at Urbana-Champaign recently piloted an undergraduate course entitled "Production, Retrieval, and Evaluation of Scientific Knowledge." The course, developed to improve the understanding of scientific information, is one of the growing number of information literacy courses offered through the university's Graduate School of Library and Information Science. The course is taught predominantly through the research and analysis of various case studies and their political and social impact on society. After the cases are presented to the class, either through a publication or a guest lecturer, the students are assigned a "problem-solving exercise" that is applicable to the case study. As students complete the necessary additional research, they get to practice their newly learned information retrieval techniques. Finally, each student takes a different viewpoint of the case study, researches publications, and prepares an argument. Each case study is then discussed and debated at the next class meeting. This type of learning makes abstract concepts more realistic because it connects the concepts to actual events.[27]

Biology

In 1985, the Philadelphia College of Pharmacy and Science, in cooperation with its library faculty, implemented a resource-based approach to required biology courses. The goal of the biology faculty was to begin acquainting students with the scientific literature in their freshman year. For example, the first semester assignment is designed to familiarize the students with such major scientific resources as *Biological Abstracts, Index Medicus, Biological and Agricultural Index,* and *Science Citation Index.* To make sure the students understand the literature, the second semester course requires them to write original abstracts on two of the articles they retrieved during the first semester.

Upper-level biology courses also use resource-based learning by expanding the students' use of available resources. For example, as students learn searching strategies for the online databases MEDLINE and Biosis, their ability to access scientific literature is reinforced. The final assignment, which includes an oral presentation, is a research paper that must be enhanced with graphics, overheads, and slides. Presentation techniques are taught in a seminar class in cooperation with the library's learning resource center.[28]

St. John's University in Minnesota also incorporated resource-based learning into its biology curriculum when it introduced "Biological Literature," a course designed to develop essential scientific writing skills. Taught collaboratively by a biology instructor and a librarian, the course meets for nine one-hour sessions. During these sessions, students are required to do several brief homework assignments, an oral report of a reviewed journal, and a bibliography on a topic of choice.[29] The objectives of the course are

- to have students learn how to search online
- to formulate criteria for the selection of materials
- to retrieve desired material
- to understand the relationship among the library catalog, other online services, the Internet, and the campus network
- to make efficient use of library services

Biology faculty at California Polytechnic State University in San Luis Obispo took a different approach to a biological literature course. They integrated current medical and scientific stories covered by the news media with the core curriculum of search strategies and critical thinking. For example, after students review a news story, they must identify the access points they would use to verify the facts. The students then review the sources to be used as references. Once they have read the reference articles, the students scrutinize the articles for any discrepancies.

This unique course is taught in the format of the game *Jeopardy*. Students must quickly answer questions arranged in certain categories. Students consistently give the course's approach high evaluation marks. Faculty are convinced the course contributes significantly to the students' abilities to be skeptical readers of the popular press.[30]

SOCIOLOGY

Deborah A. Abowitz, an associate professor of sociology and the associate dean of faculty in the College of Arts and Sciences at Bucknell University in Lewisburg, Pennsylvania, worked cooperatively with the campus librarians to develop courses and assignments in sociology that are geared towards advancing students' research skills, especially as those skills pertain to electronic information retrieval.

During an introductory course, students are assigned various sociological concepts. They are then required to do an online literature search and choose an article that summarizes an assigned sociological concept; however, the summary must include ideas discussed in the class and the textbook. The instructor monitors the process students use by checking their progress every few weeks. To complete the assignment, the students must submit a printed copy of their literature search as well as a copy of the article. Students accomplish the following course objectives with just this one assignment:

- do online literature searches
- manage their workload
- write clearly by limiting the length of the paper to one page
- synthesize knowledge from various sources, such as lectures, textbooks, and online sources[31]

WORLD CIVILIZATION

LeMoyne College in Syracuse, New York, has a straightforward approach to the coverage of traditional research skills in a "Western and World Civilization" core course that is required for all freshmen and most transfers. The goal and objectives of the course are as follows:

> **Goal:** Students will develop their own search strategies based on an understanding of the processes used for gathering information to complete class assignments, to prepare reports, or to do research projects.
>
> **Objectives:**
>
> 1. To develop a thesis statement for a research project by using information sources to gain an understanding of a topic.
>
> 2. To be aware of the difference between primary and secondary sources.
>
> 3. To understand the bibliographic and organizational structure of information sources and to evaluate sources based on structure.
>
> 4. To understand how information sources are intellectually accessed.
>
> 5. To understand how information sources are physically organized and accessed.[32]

Washington State University received a grant from the National Endowment for the Humanities to develop an interdisciplinary World Civilization curriculum that was targeted for freshmen. Faculty from various disciplines and librarians served on the steering committee to develop two courses that would give students a general background in social studies and an introduction to research skills. The course highlights various media, such as films, slides, and audio and print materials. The librarians also emphasized "event" attendance, i.e., students were expected to attend cultural exhibitions at their institutions and discuss their experiences.[33]

During the first semester, students cover question analysis and investigative skills along with some basic research instruction. During the second semester, after students learn about the location and evaluation of various resource materials, they are required to write a bibliographic essay, the grade for which is included in the final mark for the course.

CONCLUSION

The most difficult aspect of writing this chapter was bringing it to a close. I become aware of another positive step in establishing or advancing information literacy efforts almost every day—through reading a journal, receiving an e-mail message, or talking with a colleague. The fairly rapid development of such efforts creates a certain frustration; information on resource-based learning acquired when this book was written most likely does not capture the full nature of that same effort today.

This chapter, therefore, ends with hearty encouragement for each campus and academic program to do its own occasional literature searches to network with those on other campuses who have similar interests and concerns. Reinventing the wheel is never needed because librarians involved in planning information literacy programs never have any trouble forging connections.

Although such models can be valuable planning tools, the best approach for academic leaders is to start with existing models on one's own campus and build from there. Enthusiastic faculty are the best evangelists for information literacy, and the closer to home they are, the more effective they will be. Also, when campus colleagues speak about more exciting class discussions, better student research, and more stimulating presentations by their students, they have a far more sympathetic audience than any outside expert could expect. Ultimately, the information literacy evangelists and the new converts can collectively look for models from other campuses to enrich their own efforts to integrate information literacy effectively throughout their departmental offerings.

NOTES

Epigraph: Nolan Bowie, "Equity and Access to Information Technology," *The Annual Review* (1990), 135.

1. Bruce D. Friedman, Dane Ward, and Art Biagianti, "Enhancing Student Ability to Navigate the Rapidly Changing Informaiton Environment," Wayne State University, Detroit, MI, 1995, 1-2.
2. Ibid., 5.
3. Ibid., 6-7.
4. Jan Kennedy Olsen and Bill Coons, "Cornell University's Information Literacy Program," *Coping with Information Literacy: Bibliographic Instruction for the Information Age,* edited by Linda Sharato (Ann Arbor, MI: Pierian Press, 1989).
5. Blake Ives and Sirkka L. Jarvenpaa, "Will the Internet Revolutionize Business Education and Research?" *Sloan Management Review,* 37 (Spring 1996), 33.
6. Douglass K. Hawes, "Information Literacy and the Business Schools," *Journal of Education for Business,* 70 (September/October, 1994), 54.
7. Peter Drucker, "Be Data Literate—Know What to Know," *The Wall Street Journal* (December 1, 1992), 16:3.
8. Vaughan C. Judd and Betty J. Timms, "Integrating Bibliographic Instruction into a Marketing Curriculum: A Hands-On Workshop Approach Using Interactive Team-Teaching," *Reference Services Review,* 24 (Spring 1996), 21-30.
9. Taken from information submitted by the University of Maryland Eastern Shore, Department of Business and Economics, in response to a 1994/1995 survey regarding information literacy programs conducted by the Commission on Higher Education of the Middle States Association of Colleges and Schools, the Western Association of Schools and Colleges, and the Association of College and Research Libraries.

10. Barbara MacAdam, "Information Literacy: Models for the Curriculum," *College & Research Libraries News*, 10 (November, 1990), 949.

11. Ibid., 948-51.

12. Richard Knaub, "Confessions of a Former Scenic Designer," in *A Colorado Response to the Information Society: The Changing Academic Library*, edited by Patricia Senn Breivik (Bethesda, MD, 1983) ERIC, ED 269 017, 193, 40-43.

13. H. Stephen McMinn, "Information Literacy Proposal, College of Engineering," Wayne State University, Detroit, MI, January 31, 1997, [photocopy].

14. Colette O. Holmes, D. Elizabeth Irish, and Thomas C. Haley, "BI for an Undergraduate Engineering Course: An Interactive Model for a Large-Enrollment Course," *Research Strategies*, 12 (Spring 1994), 115-21.

15. Marygrove College, Detroit, MI, brochures received from LOEX Clearinghouse, Ypsilanti, MI.

16. Marianne Gaunt and Stan Nash, "Expository Writing and Information Literacy: A Pilot Project," *Information Literacy: Developing Students as Independent Learners, New Directions for Higher Education*, No. 78, edited by D. W. Farmer and Terrence F. Mech (San Francisco: Jossey-Bass Publishers, Summer 1992), 83-90.

17. Marvin E. Wiggins, "Information Literacy at Universities: Challenges and Solutions," *Information Literacy: Developing Students as Independent Learners, New Directions for Higher Education*, No. 78, edited by D.W. Farmer and Terrence F. Mech (San Francisco: Jossey-Bass Publishers, Summer 1992), 73-81.

18. "Project Phoenix: Rekindling the Intellectual Adventure for the 21st Century," a report by the San Jose State University Foundation, San Jose, CA, 1996.

19. Anita Kay Lowry, "Beyond BI: Information Literacy in the Electronic Age," *Research Strategies*, 8 (Winter 1990), 22-27.

20. "Neef Law Library Teams Up with Law School on Special Research Sessions for Students," *Wayne State University Library System Newsletter*, 37 (1996), 11.

21. Kathryn J. Hannah, Marion J. Ball, and Margaret J. A. Edwards, *Introduction to Nursing Informatics* (New York: Springer-Verlag, 1994), 4.

22. Edward L. Anderson, "Technology for Consumers and Information Needs in Health Care," in *Healthcare Information Management Systems: A Practical Guide*, 2nd ed., edited by Marion J. Ball (New York: Springer-Verlag, 1995), 3.

23. Susan C. Reinhard and Patricia J. Mounton, "Integrating Informatics into the Graduate Community Health Nursing Curriculum," *Public Health Nursing*, 12, No. 3 (June, 1995), 151-58.

24. Patrick Ragains, "The Legislative/Regulatory Process and BI: A Course-Integrated Unit," *Research Strategies*, 13 (Spring 1995), 116-21.

25. Taken from information submitted by the Medical College of Georgia in response to a 1994/1995 survey regarding information literacy programs conducted by the Commission on Higher Education of the Middle States Association of Colleges and Schools, the Western Association of Schools and Colleges, and the Association of College and Research Libraries.

26. Elizabeth A. Olson, "Evidence-Based Practice: A New Approach to Teaching the Integration of Research and Practice in Gerontology," *Educational Gerontology*, 22 (1996), 523-37.

27. Brett Sutton, "Understanding Scientific Knowledge and Communication: Library and Information Science in the Undergraduate Curriculum," *Journal of Education of Library and Information Science*, 37, No. 1 (Winter 1996), 11-29.

28. John R. Porter, "Natural Partners: Resource-Based and Integrative Learning," *Information Literacy: Developing Students as Independent Learners, New Directions for Higher Education*, No. 78, edited by D.W. Farmer and Terrence F. Mech (San Francisco: Jossey-Bass Publishers, Summer 1992), 45-53.

29. Taken from information submitted by St. John's University in response to a 1994/1995 survey regarding information literacy programs conducted by the Commission on Higher Education of the Middle States Association of Colleges and Schools, the Western Association of Schools and Colleges, and the Association of College and Research Libraries.

30. Paul T. Adalian, Jr., "Use of Media News in Bibliographic Instruction: An Application in a Biological Literature Course," *What's Good Instruction Now?: Library Instruction for the 90s*, edited by Linda Sharato (Ann Arbor, MI: Pierian Press, 1993), 31-36.

31. Deborah A. Abowitz, "Developing Awareness and Use of Library Resources in Undergraduate Sociology: A Sample Assignment," *Teaching Sociology*, 22 (January, 1994), 58-64.

32. Taken from information submitted by LeMoyne College in response to a 1994/1995 survey regarding information literacy programs conducted by the Commission on Higher Education of the Middle States Association of Colleges and Schools, the Western Association of Schools and Colleges, and the Association of College and Research Libraries.

33. Paula Elliog, "The View from Square One: Librarian and Teaching Faculty Collaboration on a New Interdisciplinary Course in World Civilizations," *Integrating Library Use Skills into the General Education Curriculum* (New York: Haworth Press, 1989), 87-99.

CHAPTER 5

The Challenges of Human Resources

Information is only a precondition for equality; there must also be empowerment.

—James O'Toole

When faced with a major decision, whether personal or professional, most people today will ask advice from family, friends, or colleagues; stack up the results; and then tally the pros and cons. Unfortunately, many of these sources of information have little solid knowledge or expertise in the area of concern. As a result, the balancing of pros and cons becomes extremely complex because one has to speculate on the reliability and even the accuracy of the advice received. Only when health or legal matters are concerned, and when money is available, do people seek professional advice, and then usually from only one source of information.

The intent of this chapter is to make decision making a little easier for campus leaders weighing whether and how to pursue information literacy. Because the information presented here comes from both the literature and from those involved in information literacy initiatives, this chapter will help academic leaders benefit from the experiences of those who are already pursuing a goal of information literacy through resource-based learning on their campuses. For those who may have just made that decision, this chapter will help them better understand the challenges they will have to face to facilitate the process of helping students become information literate. Indeed, making the necessary changes and adjustments requires a major shift in how education is viewed on their campuses. For example, students must assume more responsibility for their own learning; instead of being handed carefully screened and prepackaged packets of information, students must learn to go out into the ever-growing jungle of information to find the materials they need for a particular subject. Concurrently, faculty must move from being "a sage on the stage to a guide on the side"; they must make a new and stronger commitment to the development on their campuses of a collaborative learning environment.

Would these kinds of substantial changes be worth the end result: The preparation of all students for success and lifelong learning in the twenty-first century? Because of the ultimate benefits to students and society, this question should be quickly and easily answered in the affirmative. Next, we must consider the challenges to which this commitment gives rise.

THE CHALLENGE OF OWNERSHIP

One of the first challenges that administrators have to address is facilitating a campuswide mental shift from thinking of information literacy as a library issue to understanding that it is really a learning issue. The need for this shift is somewhat illustrated by the story of railroads in the United States. Railroad executives thought they were in the railroad business, and because of that narrow focus, they never realized that they were really in the transportation business. As a result, the trucking industry was able to grow significantly, almost putting the railroads out of business. While it is true that reaching the goal of information literacy involves library information resources and services, information literacy is not so much library business as it is the business of education and, in particular, how learning takes place. Only when academic leaders and faculty see information literacy as being at the heart of their responsibilities to prepare students for lifelong learning will education in the twenty-first century be able to flourish and grow.

THE CHALLENGE FOR STUDENTS

It's not easy being a student these days. Most students suffer stress from conflicting demands in their lives, with family and work responsibilities vying with the demands of earning a college degree. Although some students enjoy playing information explorers by "surfing the net," most are far less adventuresome when it comes to courses and grades. Indeed, most would probably choose to do course work within a limited, clearly defined context. Most find security and ease in being handed instructions that explain exactly what to read, what to do, and what to learn. *How long does this paper have to be?* and *How many sources do I need to use?* are questions frequently asked by students with such an outlook on learning.

If such students are asked to assume more responsibility for their own learning, to independently find the resources from which to learn, and to work collaboratively with other students, they will probably respond with various degrees of insecurity and fear.

Faculty members can take a number of steps to help students lose their dependence on professors and assume responsibility for their own learning through resource-based learning.

- Provide clear, well-written instructions for the assignment.
- Build into the course calendar checkpoints that will assure students they are on target or will allow time for adjustments in direction.
- Assure students that their uneasiness is natural and parallels what they will encounter in their professional and personal lives.
- Assure students that the faculty member is standing in their corner to coach them to a successful completion of the work.

A department or college can also take steps to lessen student anxiety.

- Articulate the program's commitment to prepare students to be lifelong learners.
- Explain how becoming lifelong learners will affect all their learning experiences and the rest of their lives.
- Ensure a consistency in expectations among the faculty.

THE CHALLENGES FOR FACULTY

Dr. Howard Simmons, who served as executive director of the Commission on Higher Education (CHE) of the Middle States Association of Colleges and Schools until 1996 when he joined the faculty at Arizona State University, knows from personal experience that many will resist buying into information literacy.

> The task of convincing CHE that information literacy is important to the improvement of the teaching and learning process was a relatively easy feat compared to the task of convincing administrators and faculty. More difficult still is the task of convincing faculty and administrators that resource-based learning techniques are not just bureaucratic schemes dreamed up by librarians.[1]

For conscientious faculty who understand how important it is for their students to develop information literacy abilities, making a change to resource-based learning means evolving from being good teachers to being good facilitators of learning. Despite a lack of peer models and a lack of pedagogical training or personal experience with resource-based learning, they will move from being the fount of all knowledge to becoming organizers of learning experiences. For many other faculty members, a number of potential points of resistance must be addressed as efforts in resource-based learning move forward.

Overcoming Initial Faculty Resistance

The many conflicting demands on their time lead many faculty members to greet any seemingly new initiative with suspicion. At first, faculty may hope that resource-based learning is simply a new fad that will disappear before they are forced to give it any time or thought. In 1994, a comprehensive Australian study on lifelong learning documented the critical need for information literacy abilities and reported other causes of faculty resistance to resource-based learning.

> During the interviews it became clear, however, that for the majority of teaching staff information literacy was not an issue of concern. In many instances, they believed that students either already had the necessary skills of information retrieval and management or that they would "pick them up" in the course of their studies. Often they opposed vehemently any incursion by librarians or other information specialists into their slice of the curriculum, although it is hard to resist the conclusion that frequently this was because they lacked the confidence to retrieve and manage information themselves.[2]

The first step in facilitating smooth transitions to resource-based learning is to provide faculty with easily internalized information on the limitations of the lecture method and the reasons why the Information Age requires that students be prepared for lifelong learning after graduation. Ideally, faculty should be reminded of how rapidly the information in their own fields is expanding and changing and of the ongoing challenge they face in keeping abreast of new developments. Some faculty members will quickly recognize that students are even more easily overwhelmed and in great need of faculty assistance to develop the skills they also need to stay up-to-date. Such general awareness-raising efforts will create mind sets that are conducive to moving beyond standard operating procedures in the classroom.

A clearly articulated campus commitment to preparing students for lifelong learning, to developing their critical thinking skills, or to preparing them to be lifelong problem-solvers can also facilitate a positive faculty mind set. Any such commitment can easily serve as a philosophical foundation for the development of information literacy programs. In fact, information literacy efforts can become a reasonably easy sell on campus if their complementary relationships with existing undergraduate improvement efforts are pointed out.

The climate for faculty acceptance of information literacy efforts can also be enhanced by placing these efforts within the context of existing campus commitments. Rather than being sold as a new initiative, information literacy efforts can be packaged as an empowerment tool for the achievement of already agreed-upon campus priorities. For example, if freshman retention is a concern, models and successful outcomes from high school information literacy efforts can provide a basis for freshman retention initiatives including, in some situations, actual partnering with feeder high schools.*

Or, if campus energies are being directed at enhancing the general education requirements, exploring how information literacy can enhance academic success and lifelong learning for all students should be a natural tie-in. Of course, any subject-specific curriculum review would offer similar opportunities. The important factor is not to promote information literacy as an end in itself, but as a means to strengthen existing and already shared academic commitments.

Another way to integrate information literacy efforts into existing endeavors is to incorporate them into assessment considerations. For example, when accreditation self-studies are undertaken, library information resources and services can be integrated throughout the report with emphasis on how they are being used to support campus achievement of its mission and goals.

Impact on Faculty Research Time

The publish-or-perish reward system in higher education forces faculty to stay current within their own focused research areas. This system promotes and even encourages teaching that reflects faculty research priorities so as to minimize time taken from research. At least initially, faculty will need additional time to plan how to better incorporate information resources and technology into their courses. However, even when the start-up phase is over, faculty will need to continue making time to consult with information specialists on campus to keep up-to-date with the ever-changing information resources and technology in their field. If such expenditures of time are seen as being counterproductive to achieving promotion and tenure, faculty will have little incentive to support the establishment of resource-based learning programs.

If faculty members are isolated from the information experts on their campuses, they will never have the time or the desire to work for the changes needed to adopt resource-based learning. Instead, faculty members need to have adequate support from librarians and other information specialists. In

---

*An illustration of such a partnering is the designation of an outreach librarian, Deborah Tucker, in the Wayne State University Undergraduate Library, which opened in September 1997. This initiative began in the spring of 1997 when key school and campus personnel met in focus groups to determine collaborative ways of promoting earlier learning of research skills to enhance college retention and academic success. Tucker now spends half her time working with school library media specialists and teachers from WSU's feeder schools to develop teacher workshops, plan curriculum enhancements, and facilitate teacher use of university resources. This collaboration will transform the high school trip to an academic library from a boring walk through a bewildering maze of information resources to an exciting strategy for developing competence and confidence in library use.

addition to ensuring such enhanced support levels, campus administrators also need to make sure that faculty development efforts and reward systems make clear that resource-based learning is important and will be suitably acknowledged.

Faculty Control of Student Learning

For many years, the expected format for higher education courses has been for professors to lecture, assign readings, and evaluate the content of papers. Because students seldom have the desire or time to go beyond the requirements, professors could be fairly certain that they knew more than their students knew. However, some professors may fear that the introduction of resource-based learning will send students out into the wide universe of information to read some prestigious expert who disagrees with what has been taught in class or find some information more current than last week's lecture.

Such fears can only be overcome through experience with resource-based learning and a gradual acceptance of the concept that professors need not know everything as long as they know how to find relevant information. Disagreements among experts afford a great opportunity for students to learn how to evaluate conflicting information from various authoritative sources. Students will use this skill throughout their entire lives.

Finding Good Models to Emulate

The potential role for faculty in supporting students' abilities to access, evaluate, and effectively use information is often not immediately evident because there exists a strong, long-standing model that excludes any systematic development of students' research skills. In 1980, an English professor and former provost at Earlham College vividly described this typical model.

> What has been our experience as professors, after all? We have been accustomed to having the toughest courses we took and the toughest we teach introduce the longest list of books on reserve. Our professors gave us fine annotated bibliographies and we may do the same for our students. Often it has been our experience that the most challenging graduate seminars we took specified both the paper topics and the works we were to consult for all but the final paper; and frequently the final paper was an outgrowth of one of the shorter papers we did under instruction. That is to say, our best graduate courses in our discipline, like the best undergraduate courses we expected to teach, gave exclusive attention to mastering the content of major works in our field. Except in the rarest cases we were taught to regard the library solely as the place where all those things should be waiting for us.
>
> I think of my very good experiences with reference services in college and graduate school, but I recall that I, and everyone else I

knew, tended to go to the reference desk as a last resort and that I asked questions with no notion that I might learn a generalizable method of research which could help me become more expert in research and conceive of more interesting questions to pursue, either on my own or with the help of a reference librarian. And, I would add, I do not believe I ever thought of a librarian as a teacher until I began to work at Earlham. . . . Each piece of study I did through college and graduate school, if it had a research dimension to it, was essentially another hit or miss, hunt and peck activity. . . . I did not know much if anything about how to branch out efficiently into a new area. My independence as a student and as a thinker was consequently very limited, and I didn't even recognize the fact. I thought of the library as a vast reserve collection where I could find what had been assigned or suggested.

I suggest that my experience is not untypical of both undergraduate and graduate use of the library even now. If I am right in this, it would follow that many of us who are now teaching in colleges and universities are only slightly at home in libraries.[3]

The best place to look for models of resource-based learning is on campus. Faculty development officers and librarians should be able to identify faculty who can offer workshops or mentor other faculty interested in moving toward a resource-based learning approach to student learning. If enough faculty members cannot be found on campus, consider importing faculty from other campuses for information-gathering purposes and for faculty development offerings, or consider taking a team of people to campuses where resource-based learning is well established. Many of the examples given throughout this book would be a starting point for the latter.

Making a Long-Term Commitment to Resource-Based Learning

Overcoming faculty resistance to resource-based learning and trying some new collaborative efforts with librarians and other colleagues are not enough. Care and support needs to be ongoing to create a positive climate that fosters a growing faculty commitment.

It really doesn't take a lot to make people feel good about who they are and what they are doing and to give them confidence that they are doing a good job. With a little time and creativity, appropriate incentives can be devised to foster information literacy programs on campus. Listed below is a range of inexpensive activities to encourage faculty cooperation.

- Hold special retreats that focus on information literacy programs involving both faculty and librarians. In a multi-campus situation, hold the retreats on a systemwide basis.

- Create a program of small grant awards for teams of faculty and information specialists who integrate resource-based learning with some aspect of the curriculum.
- Highlight successful programs in campus newsletters, as part of teacher award ceremonies, etc.
- Create an annual information literacy award.
- Become involved with such programs as the American Association for Higher Education's Teaching/Learning Roundtables, which allow teams of people from campuses to look at the role of information resources and technology in curriculum reform.
- Make sure that a librarian or faculty member who has had experience with resource-based learning is included on general education committees, assessment committees, etc.
- Model faculty/librarian cooperation by having librarians do a literature search on any new administrative concern before the Council of Deans or for any new initiative on campus.

As the previous suggestions show, it is important to celebrate successes. Such acknowledgments provide incentives to more and better undertakings and provide important models that other faculty can adopt or adapt. Such celebrations also build confidence, and, like the old adage says, "Nothing breeds confidence like success."

Building Faculty Commitment

Educators have some legitimate reasons for being uncomfortable with the move to resource-based learning. Prime among these is the natural concern for student success. Because faculty are usually dealing with a field of knowledge that is expanding rapidly, they already feel pressured by the limitation of course time to cover the subject matter and perceive lectures as an efficient, if not effective, means of transferring information. The need to include group work, an important part of resource-based learning, will only heighten this concern. With this added time demand, faculty will feel unable to cover all the material needed for their students to move into a more advanced course or to pass some certification requirement.

The best strategy to win faculty over is two-pronged. First, share the research on how little knowledge students retain from lectures. Second, get faculty members to consider how rapidly information is being generated in their own fields, and the implications this overly rich information environment will have on how their students will need to work and live throughout their lives. Capitalize on the genuine concern faculty have for their students' well-being in and beyond the college years. Show faculty how resource-based learning offers a better alternative for preparing students for lifelong success.

Also suggest that faculty members keep careful documentation on student performance, tracking students' current achievements and then contrasting those achievements to the results gained by a fully developed resource-based learning approach. The results of such classroom research will strengthen faculty commitment to resource-based learning by convincing them of the big student payoff such an approach offers.

Building Faculty Confidence

Because most current faculty received their degrees prior to the information and technology explosions, they have had little or no training, and, therefore, have developed little or no confidence in the use of new information technologies. They also have had little experience as learners in classes where the use of information resources and technologies are integrated into the curriculum. This lack of first-hand experience is exacerbated for educators whose real commitment is to a discipline rather than to student learning, which by its nature must be more process than content oriented. Moreover, because both information resources and technologies are constantly and rapidly changing, integrating them more fully into the curriculum does not make for stability in course offerings.

If faculty are to foster information literacy abilities in their courses, many will need to have their own abilities enhanced. Information technology seems the easiest point at which to gain general acceptance by faculty of their need for additional skills and knowledge. Professors lose no face when they admit that they cannot teach students how to do a hyper-media project, understand the provisions of the copyright act, or set up a web page. The rapid pace of technological change means everyone needs continual updating and renewing. Many faculty would also benefit from opportunities to develop the critical-thinking components of information literacy.

Other faculty developmental needs should center around how to rethink the structure of classes and assignments to help faculty members feel comfortable with their change in roles from information provider to information facilitator. If possible, they should be able to observe or partner with peers who are already more actively engaging students in their own learning.

Last, but not least, faculty development initiatives need to target opportunities to help faculty keep up with new information resources and technology in their own fields so that they can do their own research better and feel more comfortable in aggressively engaging their own students in research.

Ongoing Faculty Development

Funds for faculty development are limited, and the ability to give release time is even more limited. Moreover, faculty interest in information literacy, even when genuine and deep, must also compete with a variety of other faculty development needs, such as assessment, collaborative learning, multiculturalism, and internationalization. However, because the need for faculty development is so important, it requires the most thoughtful, careful planning.

A well-thought-out, multi-dimensional faculty development strategy must be developed and made available to all faculty members. Such efforts could encompass the following items:

- Keep faculty apprised of new information resources and services in their own fields of research.
- Familiarize faculty with relevant resources and services beyond their areas of specialization.
- Familiarize faculty and their assistants and secretaries with the time-saving tools and services of the library.
- Help faculty understand the research capabilities and needs of their students.
- Work with faculty in developing learning experiences based on the use of books, magazines, newspapers, online and media resources, etc.
- Work with faculty in structuring experiences that will effectively promote the mastery of information literacy abilities.

The first three activities directly promote faculty comfort with the use of library resources and services. The last three activities, although directed at student learning, will promote the same ends, as faculty and librarians work and learn together while developing and offering resource-based learning experiences.

Faculty Guides

Good faculty guides, although time consuming and difficult to produce, can significantly increase the reach and depth of faculty development efforts. Such guides can be one of the best ways to support faculty integration of information resources and technologies into the curriculum. A well-conceived and easy-to-use guide will provide faculty members with a series of options for customizing information literacy to fit their particular students and their course objectives.

The Seattle Community College District prepared an unusually good example of such a guide for its instructors. The following is excerpted from the beginning of the guide and provides an explanation as to the value to students of integrating information-seeking skills into the curriculum and the importance of instructors accepting a new approach to teaching.

Including information seeking and evaluating skills in your curriculum will help students to develop critical abilities through the discovery and use of appropriate information sources. This process will require them to develop their curiosity and discover for themselves the nature of information in formats relevant to their course work and appropriate to their learning styles. It will teach them to develop strategies to find information, to challenge the credibility of sources, and to develop confidence in using resources available to them both in and beyond the library.

All of this is increasingly important when information technology is changing rapidly. Students who do not develop good abilities as information consumers now will be disadvantaged in their personal and work lives later. The more information seeking and evaluating abilities they develop in the relative safety of the college environment, the better prepared they will be to succeed in their future educational, social, and work environments.

Students need to find information to solve problems and answer questions. Often in the past students have been asked to find information to satisfy the requirements of canned exercises. It is hard for students to then apply the same skills in context when they are needed. They will retain information literacy abilities better when they practice them to satisfy real information needs. Similarly, if you hand a student a textbook and ask them to learn the material it contains, they are practicing a certain kind of learning: they should be getting an overview of the subject, they may be learning to identify what the author thinks is important, what you the instructor want them to learn, and they are asked to find answers to questions and to solve problems by finding information. They are practicing critical thinking skills and they are practicing your discipline by learning about the reference and periodical sources for your discipline, they are learning the language of your discipline, and the ways scholars in your discipline do research and communicate their results.[4]

The Seattle Community College District guide then succinctly walks faculty through

- the importance of identifying appropriate information literacy objectives
- a range of information literacy objectives appropriate for community college students from which faculty can pick and choose
- a list of approaches to incorporating information literacy into the course
- lists of desired learning outcomes for students by program and level (e.g., students in professional technical programs to adult basic education students, etc.)

- a step-by-step process for designing effective information literacy assignments[5]

The guide ends with a series of assignments for building generic library skills that can be easily adapted to differing subjects and different groups of students.

Such a guide helps instructors understand the range of information literacy skills students should be developing. Even more important, by providing a clear-cut process for integrating information resources and technology into academic courses, the guide puts professors in control, allowing them to easily and intellectually make successful changes. Finally, the guide eliminates surprises, allowing faculty to refine and expand their options by working comfortably with librarians.

Such guides would vary significantly, depending on the type of school. For example, a liberal arts college and a major university would want far more included on critical thinking and resource evaluation than a community college might want, but the various components included and the general approach taken provide a valuable model for guidebooks on all campuses. Such a guide can also provide planning for information literacy across the curriculum of an academic program or across the entire curriculum of the campus.

Faculty Assessment

There is a potential disincentive for teachers to participate in resource-based learning programs on campuses where teaching is a significant factor in promotion and tenure considerations and where student evaluations are the major factor in teaching evaluation. Unless all faculty in a particular department are engaged in resource-based learning practices, students may well not appreciate the extra involvement required in the resource-based learning courses over the more passive lectures-plus-textbook option in other courses. Because students may not realize the value of more active learning until after graduation, some students are likely to grade down on course evaluations or avoid the more demanding courses.

Current efforts to enhance both student learning and to more effectively assess teaching performance will create a healthier climate for the adoption of resource-based learning practices. For example, teaching portfolios that include samples of the students' work give evidence of the development of information management and critical thinking skills. This type of assessment can create incentives to move toward resource-based learning.

THE CHALLENGES FOR LIBRARIANS

The introduction of resource-based learning will also change the lives of librarians. They will often have to forego direct teaching of students to become collaborators and supporters of faculty in curriculum development.

The 50-Minute Library Lecture

At the beginning of each school year, librarians respond to a flood of faculty requests for 50-minute lectures to students on research tools and resources for writing term papers. Such lectures are frustrating for librarians because students will not usually begin their research until weeks later, and research skills taught in isolation from any immediate implementation are generally not remembered for long. Despite such difficult circumstances, librarians have done their best to introduce students to some of the research tools they will need that year and all the years of their lives. Amy M. Kautzman, the head of reference at the Lamont Library at Harvard, explains how she tries to make the best out of this academically unrealistic situation.

> It is difficult, in fact impossible, to teach everything about research skills [within a particular discipline] in one 50-minute class. I compromise. In other words, I look at my audience, their needs, and their skill level, and I settle for what is the most important skill set I can teach them in the allotted time period. My agenda is twofold: one, to get through my examples as quickly as possible so the students have as much time as possible for hands-on practice time; two, to point out a fault with every tool I exhibit. I need to erode the trust students inherently have in all electronic products. I need to show that they can't take the first five citations acquired through sloppy key word searches, and trust that these articles or books will provide them with strong enough information to write quality research papers.[6]

When asked to give their usual lectures, librarians need to master a tactful "no" and then be ready to offer better alternatives. Better still, they can avoid such requests by promoting ongoing opportunities to explore with faculty ways to build upon and improve past library assignments, while moving always toward a true integration of information resources and technology with curriculum. One of the best approaches is for librarians to hold a debriefing with faculty soon after students have completed their term papers. Together, they can investigate how successful students were in their research and what weaknesses were evident. These joint assessments can lay the perfect foundation for determining how research learning can best be packaged and interfaced within the course.

Budgeting Librarians' Time

Librarians are hardworking people who want to serve students and faculty well; but, like everyone else these days, librarians have limited time to accomplish all the tasks demanding their attention. As resource-based programs grow, they must find time for cooperative curriculum planning with faculty, mastering classroom techniques, creating assessments suitable for resource-based learning, developing self-paced learning modules, and meeting growing library service demands caused by students and faculty making more extensive use of library resources and services.

There are no easy answers, but librarians should certainly clarify priorities within the library itself before they seek additional institutional support. If collaboration with faculty is ranked a top priority, librarians need to determine what they should quit doing to make more time available for such collaboration. It is never easy to quit doing good things to do better or more important things, although some decisions are easier than others. For example, librarians can save some time by redirecting current library/bibliographic instruction efforts to support a well-developed and coordinated campus information literacy strategy. For librarians, such a shift will mean less direct teaching of students and more curriculum collaboration with faculty; however, these changes will eventually provide a strong basis for requests for additional staffing when service demands continue to grow.

THE CHALLENGES FOR CAMPUS OFFICERS

Academic presidents, vice presidents, and deans are all vital to the success of any campus enhancement or initiative, such as the transition to resource-based learning.

Creating a Climate for Change

A positive, though frequently overlooked, means of creating a climate for change is for campus officers to model desired learning outcomes by practicing information literacy in their daily decision making. The model in the corporate world is the Chief Information Officer (CIO) who is part of the management team and who is expected to package pertinent information for projects and decision making for easy use by other executives. These modelling efforts might range from a customized portfolio of business practices and social customs to support an executive's first trip to Japan to a concise summary of national news coverage on a pending legislative issue.

In similar fashion, the library director or another librarian can be a valuable member of administrative planning teams, helping presidents and other academic officers cope with the growing burden of general administrative affairs by supplying or analyzing information.

On campuses where organizational structure, institutional climate, or personality conflicts preclude the inclusion of the library director on the administrative team, presidents could have a librarian serve as a research assistant to a select group of administrators. This arrangement would provide online searching, document delivery services, and selected dissemination of information to all the officers (i.e., a profile of interest areas is electronically matched against new literature on a regular schedule). This approach requires regular interaction between the administrators and the liaison librarian to ensure that information needs are promptly identified and met. In either case, library personnel could condense and package information for timeliness and ease of use.

At Wayne State University, the Council of Deans as well as school and college efforts have been enriched by librarians preparing selected annotated bibliographies on such topics as teaching portfolios, affirmative action, and support services for spouses of faculty being recruited. Up-front efforts to evaluate literature, identify articles with the greatest applicability to the campus, and copy the best articles to attach to annotated bibliographies have resulted in better decision making in shorter time. Establishing a standard operational practice that discourages discussion of any new undertaking before a literature search has been conducted would significantly contribute to a campus climate that promotes both effective information management and the preparation of students as effective information consumers.

Helping Staff Become Information Literate

Information literate staff members can easily access and evaluate information, make better decisions, and improve the overall effectiveness and productivity of the office. But how can staff become information literate?

Some years ago, when University of Colorado President E. Gordon Gee was concerned about how effectively staff members in the system office were using available information for planning and evaluation purposes, he asked the librarians on the Boulder campus to conduct a workshop for his staff. In preparation for the workshop, library staff interviewed members of the president's staff to identify recent projects, then they used these projects as case studies to document what relevant information the president's staff could have easily obtained from the library. One of the outcomes of the workshop was the creation of a daily delivery service between the library and the president's office to facilitate fast and dependable turnaround time on information requested by phone.

Such workshops can increase productivity throughout the campus. A good way to cut costs in times of limited resources is to reduce "information 'float' by decreasing the delay and uncertainty associated with information."[7] Librarians can hold regular workshops for faculty assistants and campus secretaries to demonstrate how library resources and services can help them perform their jobs more effectively and efficiently. For example, using a library's microfiche collection of college catalogs and the Web or First Search for telephone directories of major U.S. cities can save time and long-distance phone or mail costs. Telephone reference services or document delivery services can further enhance office performance. Moreover, faculty and administrative assistants who know how to schedule information literacy consultations, reserve audio-visual equipment, and order books can save both classroom instructors and library personnel a great deal of time and frustration.

The contribution of librarians toward helping the campus work smarter can also include grantsmanship workshops that introduce faculty to relevant library resources and give them tips on how to write good grant proposals. Power Point workshops can help administrative staff and faculty prepare more effective presentations. Librarians could also offer workshops on how to access online and Internet resources for environmental scanning. Many of these information management learning efforts might well involve partners from other units on campus, thus modelling the partnership between the information and the subject specialist. All such instructional efforts empower campus employees to work more efficiently and effectively, and everything that raises the overall awareness on campus of working smarter through better management of information will contribute to a growing climate of support for information literacy across the curriculum.

CONCLUSION

Information literacy is a goal for all people, and resource-based learning is a people-oriented process. For the goal to be effectively addressed, students, faculty, and librarians, along with other information specialists, must come together in a dynamic partnering. It is essential, therefore, that institutional leaders give the people issues the same careful attention in planning and budgeting efforts that these leaders give to other key issues, such as technology. The next chapter deals with the problems and challenges that arise out of budgeting and planning for information literacy programs.

NOTES

Epigraph: James O'Toole, "Information and Power: Social and Political Consequences of Advanced Tele/Computing Technology," *The Annual Review* (1990).

1. Howard L. Simmons, "Information Literacy and Accreditation: A Middle States Association Perspective," *Information Literacy: Developing Students as Independent Learners, New Directions for Higher Education,* No. 78, edited by D. W. Farmer and Terrence F. Mech (San Francisco: Jossey-Bass Publishers, Summer 1992), 15-16.

2. *Developing Lifelong Learners Through Undergraduate Education,* commission report No. 28, National Board of Employment, Education and Training, edited by Philip Candy, Gary Crebert, and Jane O'Leary (Australian Government Publishing Service, August, 1994).

3. Paul A. Lacey, "The Role of the Librarian in Faculty Development: A Professor's Point of View," *Library Instruction and Faculty Development: Growth Opportunities in the Academic Community,* edited by Nyal Z. Williams and Jack T. Tsukamoto (Ann Arbor, MI: Pierian Press, 1980), 20-21.

4. Karen Michaelson, "Integrating Information Literacy Across the Curriculum: An Instructor's Guide," Seattle Central Community College, (Spring 1995), 3; photocopy provided by LOEX Clearinghouse.

5. Ibid.

6. Amy M. Kautzman, "Teaching Critical Thinking: The Alliance of Composition Studies and Research Instruction," *Reference Services Review,* 24 (Fall 1996), 64.

7. Martha Boaz, *Strategies for Meeting the Information Needs of Society in the Year 2000* (Littleton, CO: Libraries Unlimited, 1981), 86.

CHAPTER 6

Institutional Challenges

To furnish the means of acquiring knowledge is the greatest benefit that can be conferred upon mankind. It prolongs life itself and enlarges the sphere of existence.

—John Adams
1735–1826

In addition to the people challenges, a number of institutional challenges must be overcome before the process of creating the information-literate citizens of tomorrow can be successful. These challenges cluster around two key needs: the need for planning an overall campus strategy for moving to resource-based learning and the need for financial resources to implement those strategic plans.

THE CHALLENGES FOR FINANCIAL SUPPORT

Sooner or later every successful initiative will expand, creating a need for more resources—both people and dollars. While some unique aspects of the resource issue relate to the growth of information literacy programs, such growth—as with all other major new curricular efforts—will require creative reallocations and perhaps additional resources.

Because the days of significant increases for new programs are over, the question comes down to what is really important. How important is the guarantee that all graduates will be competitive in today's information society? How important is it for students to become lifelong learners? The assessed importance of these goals to the campus mission will provide the framework for the tough decisions that must be made. If faculty and other campus leaders truly believe that resource-based learning is important to the human learning process for empowering quality lives and for better economic development in our communities, then decisions must be made about allocating time and funds for information literacy programs. Good things are happening in campus classrooms and libraries these days, but they may not be as important as getting students actively involved in learning how to learn. The bottom line is that campuses need to be serious about their priorities, and only when this happens will resource reallocations become possible and promising.

Personnel Needs

Finding a solution for increased personnel is often a difficult challenge because such commitments are by nature long in duration. Yet for information literacy endeavors, additional personnel are essential if the programs are to be successful. It should be noted at the outset that library services are driven by headcount, not FTE, and often include significant use by community members. Nor can the daily necessities of building collections, meeting reference needs, and conducting general business operations be ignored. Moreover, increasing responsibilities related to expanding information technologies and the need for greater networking for resource sharing are also making heavier demands on staff resources. Under these circumstances, even the best use of existing human resources will likely not allow for the increased personnel demands generated by a strong information literacy initiative.

However, even fairly modest investments in personnel can result in a significant expansion of information literacy efforts across the campus. Such investments can also provide an important margin of flexibility for academic affairs as a whole. An investment in a faculty position only improves the quality of learning in that one program, and, as student demands change, it is difficult to reallocate faculty positions from one department to another. An additional librarian position, however, has an impact across all the disciplines served by the library and is, therefore, more easily responsive to changing university priorities, especially since such a position can support information literacy in several disciplines. (Librarian positions are also particularly well suited for supporting general education and multi-disciplinary efforts.) As a result, librarian positions provide greater flexibility for responding to future needs.

In many cases, the need is less for librarians than for paraprofessional and technical support staff who can relieve higher paid librarians from the daily business or more technical operations of their responsibilities. The latter, while important, do not require professional training, and the librarian's time is thus freed to direct more important information literacy efforts. Although salaries will vary according to the various positions, personnel and fringe benefit dollars will likely go further when directed at library support and technical staff positions rather than at new faculty positions, especially considering 9- versus 12-month appointments.

Despite these budgetary and service benefits, such changes will require thoughtful and delicate academic leadership. For example, the robust nature of the information literacy program at California State University at San

Marcos, which has already been described, is partially the result of Provost Richard Millman's willingness to allocate two new positions to support the program in 1995.[1]

The Need for New Technology

The financial issues regarding information resources and information technology are hard to separate. The vast majority of information literacy abilities still exist apart from newer technology, and can therefore be developed without use of technology. However, some information can only be accessed via computer, and the ease of access to such information is being greatly enhanced. Moreover, the current small fraction of information available online will grow significantly as the information explosion continues. Therefore, adequate information technology is essential.

A serious commitment to information literacy certainly has serious implications for campus technology. Such a commitment necessitates the identification and establishment of resource and service priorities to effectively promote faculty and student use of a wide range of information resources as an integrated part of the learning process.

Information literacy places people's needs at the top of such a priority list. It requires that information resources and technologies be accessible, user friendly, and coordinated. It requires that information resources be integrated and networked so that faculty members can use all the resources and services that support the particular learning objectives of their courses. With the demands placed on faculty, it is unrealistic to expect them to go to separate service areas for computing, library, and media services.

Similarly, if information literacy is a goal for all students, then students must have access to computers for self-directed use, and training opportunities and software must be available to facilitate their use of computers and networks. Students must also have continual practice—both as a part of the curriculum and as a part of their extra-curricular activities—in accessing and using information successfully in all its formats. Both faculty and students must have ready access to information systems 24 hours a day, seven days a week, from dorm rooms, homes, offices, and classrooms.

Collaboration with librarians is especially beneficial during the planning for technology. As far back as 1984, President Alan E. Guskin and colleagues at the University of Wisconsin at Parkside pointed out the unique qualification that librarians have for such a role.

> Further, librarians—at least the effective ones—in their efforts to serve the needs of faculty members and their disciplines, have developed an understanding of faculty information needs across the campus through interviews with faculty, working with faculty on collection development.... performing online database searches, etc. In fact, it is probably true that the staff of the library have a better sense of the intellectual

needs of the entire faculty, or any significant segment, than any other group on a university campus. This university-wide perspective has enabled them to plan the university's collection needs and will enable the library to effectively serve the university as the faculty become more attuned to the power of computer and micro-computer applications.[2]

Specifically, besides additional funding through reallocations from other campus areas or donor contributions, the best means of addressing technology needs related to information literacy is to make wise decisions regarding technology. However, based upon the number of conference programs and articles written about technology planning, the issue seems far from being resolved.

Student Resource Needs

According to Lorie Roth, director of academic services and professional development for the California State University System, students must have "a wide variety of information resources that challenges their minds, encourages them to read and research broadly, and makes them aware of the range and breadth of the knowledge developed by many people and many cultures."[3] Roth is not in any way advocating the bean counting approach to inhouse library collections that is epitomized by assessment systems that value the number of volumes over considerations of how much and how wisely students and faculty use the materials. Instead, Roth acknowledges that "static or declining budgets, coupled with high inflationary rates, have greatly affected libraries and reduced access to knowledge for students." She urges that "Campus information infrastructure must be restored and maintained in order for students to be exposed to the broad range of information and knowledge necessary for a college or university education and for the full development of information management skills."[4]

One specific area holds significant potential for savings—cuts in journal titles that support the research of few or even single faculty members. Of course, this is a sensitive area because the mere mention of cutting any journals is abhorrent to most faculty. The truth of the matter is that many journals are bought just in case they are needed. Fortunately, breakthroughs in information technology are providing levels of access to information on demand that were barely dreamed of a decade ago. Unfortunately, the emotional need of faculty members to have "their" journals on the shelves is difficult to overcome.

For purposes of information literacy, this issue of journals is of importance for two reasons. First, in the real world, graduates will not have all journals needed for research available in their homes or offices; therefore, students—while still in school—must gain significant experience finding needed information from many sources and obtaining it electronically, for that is what they will have to do after they graduate. Second, when academic leaders set the tone for faculty working cooperatively with librarians to explore access alternatives to ownership, significant dollar savings can result. These savings can be translated both into increasing staffing to support information literacy programs and providing electronic document delivery systems that can benefit all faculty and students. Unfortunately, librarians cannot take such initiative by themselves; they need strong support from more forward-looking faculty and academic administrators.

Another related idea for additional funding comes from the K-12 level. In the following excerpt, Janadene Harvey, an Iowa City principal, explains her decision to stop buying basal textbooks and use that money to support resource-based learning:

> I guess one issue that we often tend to avoid is that we put substantial amounts of money into the purchasing of basal reading programs in all our schools throughout the nation. Until we begin to look at redirecting or reallocating some of that money into materials that would be supportive of thematic units, we're not going to go very far because there are not going to be lots of dollars that can be added to the budget for resource-based learning.
>
> But clearly nationwide, we've spent millions of dollars providing every child with a basal reader, and yet what we really have come to realize is that we don't need to do every story in a basal reader, we don't need to do the stories in the sequence they appear, and we don't need to do every chapter test. When that realization occurs, you then look at the cost of implementing the basal reading program, and you must conclude that clearly here are some dollars that can be reallocated. . . . How much money would you have to put into learning resources if you quit buying basal readers and perhaps even some textbooks?[5]

Harvey's final question was also asked by Dr. Darrell W. Krueger, president of Winona State University and part of an effort by the Minnesota State University System Task Force to define the academic library of the future. A three-year study that involved a broad representation of personnel from across the campuses of the MSU system gave much attention to how academic libraries could support student learning. It was in this context that President Krueger asked the challenging question about the amount of resources that could be available if the average student cost for textbooks each semester was redirected into campus information resources! Revolutionary as that may sound, it is worth thinking about.

THE CHALLENGES FOR PLANNING

Initial plans for incorporating information literacy programs can assume that some of the demands required for effectively integrating information resources and technology into the curriculum can be absorbed by faculty and staff realigning their resources. However, such reallocations, of even such commodities as time, can go only so far. In addition, successful information literacy programs eventually result in ever-increasing demands on computer, library, and media services. This success is, of course, highly desirable, but it also creates additional budgetary demands. Thus, careful upfront planning cannot be overemphasized.

Beginning Planning for Resource-Based Learning

Once the institutional climate that supports integrating information resources and technology into the curriculum is created and disincentives are eliminated, or at least reduced, efforts need to be directed toward preparing for a long-term commitment to information literacy efforts. Unfortunately, a major weakness on most campuses is that programs are frequently ad hoc in nature. As a result, successful offerings disappear when a faculty member moves to another campus, or students' opportunities depend on which faculty member happens to teach the section they are assigned.

An important long-term strategy is to institutionalize all information literacy efforts. The models described in this chapter from campuses across the United States will supply an overall vision of how to begin and what to do after that. At the initial stages of developing a strategy, some designated or voluntary trailblazers must forge a path for others to follow. When a campus sets information literacy as its goal, librarians can well serve as the trailblazers because they can help faculty formulate successful information literacy programs by setting clear objectives and then offering practical steps to facilitate the plans that are made. Librarians at Wayne State University, for example, used the following practical working concepts as a reminder of where the campus was headed.

Information Literacy: A Student's Perspective

As I develop essential information literacy, I must learn how to analyze and identify my information needs; locate the information my needs demand by using a wide range of resources and strategies; evaluate the information I have found to determine its appropriateness to my specific needs as well as its reliability, bias, completeness, and timeliness; and use the information to meet my needs.

The Three Commandments for Library Instruction

- Focus on what is being learned, not what is being taught.
- Create opportunities for active learning, not occasions for passive attendance.
- Remember that your goal is the development of Lifelong Learners, not merely students who understand the minutia of doing research in your library.[6]

Using these clearly stated objectives, the information literacy team leaders acknowledged that the ideals of course-integrated information literacy and information literacy across the curriculum could not be achieved overnight, but the leaders believed that they could be accomplished strategically and incrementally. Primary in their early efforts were the following objectives aimed at promoting faculty collaboration:

- We will identify specific instructors, courses, and programs open to collaboration with librarians and work with them to truly integrate Information Literacy into the curriculum.
- We will identify academic and professional groups that have learning goals related to information management and critical thinking for members of their professions and discuss those standards with the academic programs that prepare students for said professions.
- We will work with targeted faculty to identify the information competencies they would like their students to possess and to determine the stages in which their students will develop these competencies. Information Literacy should be developed in a sequence of class experiences throughout degree programs with each building on the previous while avoiding needless repetition.
- We will, in our interactions with the faculty, exemplify Robert Greenleaf's concept of "servant leadership."[7]

Including Faculty in the Planning Process

Librarians can significantly facilitate the campus adoption of well-conceived programs by drafting policies and learning outcomes or competencies statements for guiding the development of campus information literacy programs. However, little will result from such efforts unless there is significant faculty buy-in to such policies and learning outcome statements. In recent years, such statements have begun to appear, but the results of a survey published in 1992 showed that few of the libraries responding "had any policy on user education."[8]

Whenever possible, faculty should be involved from the beginning in the development of instructional policies and statements of learning outcomes for information literacy. Starting with good models already developed with faculty involvement at other campuses can be extremely helpful—such as the following list of core competencies that was developed by faculty and librarians for the California State University System.

- Define the research topic.
- Determine the information requirements for the research question, problem, or issue.

- Locate and retrieve relevant information.
- Use the technological tools for accessing information.
- Evaluate information.
- Organize and synthesize information.
- Communicate using a variety of information technologies.
- Understand the ethical, legal, and socio-political issues surrounding information and information technology.
- Use, evaluate, and treat critically information received from the mass media.
- Judge the product and the process.[9]

Librarians at the University of Maryland Eastern Shore (UMES), a campus committed to the development of student library skills, took a different approach to building broad-based faculty involvement. They appealed directly to the faculty and administration by asking for their help and by confessing that by themselves they could not successfully reach the goals set for information literacy. They then asked a series of questions (some of which are listed below) regarding individual faculty members' involvement in the integration of research-based assignments, or, more specifically, their involvement in the "Bibliographic Instruction and Information Literacy" program at UMES.

- List one or more Information Literacy initiatives in which you have been involved.
- Highlight one or two basic strategies that you used.
- State any problems that you have encountered.
- List two or more successful outcomes.[10]

Not only did these questions produce more interaction between faculty and librarians, but they also were the catalyst for a positive initiative with faculty (i.e., you are important to these efforts and we know you are probably already doing good things). Based upon the responses to the questions, the librarians were able to identify potential role models/mentors from among the faculty and to identify successful initiatives upon which to build additional efforts.

The UMES approach to integrating information resources and technology into the curriculum falls short of the more comprehensive programs of information literacy advocated in this book because UMES's program is properly labeled "Bibliographic Instruction." The course description emphasizes the reference tools to be taught rather than student mastery of information literacy abilities. Nevertheless, the well-thought-out strategic plan developed at UMES can be easily adjusted to a plan including more ambitious information literacy programs. Such a plan would contain the following components:

- a mission statement
- a description of the program

- a purpose
- goals and options
- a description of clientele and marketing for reaching them
- an evaluation plan
- a description of three suggested levels of instruction[11]

An even more detailed strategic plan for information literacy enhancement was developed at Griffith University in Queensland, Australia. This plan includes three strategies targeted at staff development, curricular development, and extra-curricular education. The university's plan states that "these three strategies are supported by a central strategy or coordinating focus on information literacy and information literacy education,"[12] as illustrated by Figure 6-1.

Campuses that want to move ahead aggressively or even just effectively with information literacy need to undertake both curricular planning and serious implementation/strategy planning. Moreover, this kind of planning works best with the active involvement of faculty, librarians, faculty development officers, and media and academic computing personnel. However, as good as such library-initiated plans are, unless there is a faculty buy-in and support by chairs, deans, and academic vice presidents to institutionalize literacy efforts, little progress will actually be made.

A Multi-Campus Model for Resource-Based Learning

Given the conflicting demands on the time of faculty and librarians, collaborative efforts that span more than one campus would be capable of producing efficiencies in effort; multi-campus models would also seem useful for community colleges, university systems, and other groups of campuses to explore.

California State University (CSU) is an important multi-campus model for resource-based learning. It could be used as an in-depth case study of the development and implementation of a complex information literacy program that got everyone asking the right questions. Moreover, the CSU program accomplished its goal in a setting that involves a wide diversity of students and institutions that are under the constraints of limited resources, a common situation on most campuses today. The CSU efforts to date exemplify a number of characteristics, listed below, that fall somewhere on the continuum of helpful to necessary in the development of programs—whether in a multi-campus situation or a single institution.

- Enjoys support at all levels.
- Involves faculty from all disciplines.
- Is concerned with student achievement.

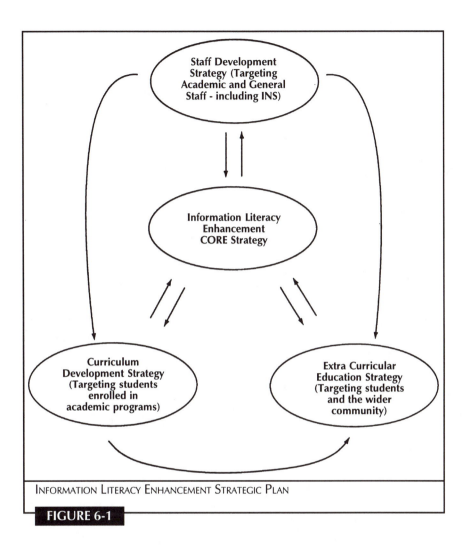

INFORMATION LITERACY ENHANCEMENT STRATEGIC PLAN

FIGURE 6-1

- Builds in student assessment.
- Has a strong theoretical base but is results oriented.
- Fosters collaboration among faculty and librarians.

System-level attention to this strong initiative at CSU began in 1994 when the initiatives of the systemwide council of library directors and the systemwide commission on technology addressed the following question: In the Information Age of the 1990s, do our students know how to find, evaluate, and use information? From this simple beginning, enormous campus interest developed in the information literacy needs of students. Then, with the encouragement of the new director of academic services and professional development, a CSU system staff person, the following milestones occurred:

April 1994: Established a systemwide work group consisting of chancellor's office staff, campus vice presidents for academic affairs, library directors, faculty, and other campus administrators.

November 1995: Held a systemwide conference, attended by 65 people, for discussion of issues relevant to information competence. Campuses were asked to send two representatives to the workshop: one librarian and one disciplinary faculty member.

December 1995: Published "Information Competence in the CSU: A Report."

March 1996: Began collaborative dialogues on information literacy with the other two post-secondary segments in California: the University of California and the California Community Colleges.

June 1996: Sponsored a systemwide 2-day workshop entitled "Using Information Resources, Case Studies, and Other Strategies in Promoting Active Learning." Attended by 23 faculty from around the system.

June 1996: Funded a $67,000 multi-campus project to develop information competence modules to be shared among campuses.

September 1997: Allocated $10,000 to each of the 22 system campuses to be used specifically for information competence.

A model for efficient use of staff time is the $67,000 allocated in June 1996 to fund a multi-campus project. Five of the system's 22 campuses were funded to collaborate on the development of Interactive Information Competency modules for applications in library credit courses and other courses within the curriculum. The project is designed to develop classroom multimedia presentations, collaborative in-class exercises, and self-paced WWW instructional models with an electronic workbook component. Discipline-specific information competencies were also identified and integrated into the modules. Anticipated outcomes from this project include the creation of a central clearinghouse for information competency by identifying non-WWW-based efforts for conversion into HTML and existing WWW Information Competency sites within the CSU for systemwide sharing of ideas. The address for this web site is http://www.lib.calpoly.edu/infocomp/index.html.

Other Collaborative Models

Not all campuses are part of multi-campus systems. Yet pooling staff resources from a few campuses to assist information literacy programs on many campuses is a good model to follow. Where formal systems do not exist, similar benefits can be gained through voluntary cooperation. Such collaboration should also be attractive for state and private funding sources concerned with getting more impact out of continuing large investments in technology. The provision of "inhouse" dollars to fund information literacy efforts should convey the importance of such undertakings.

Campus resources can also go further by tapping into external experts, clearinghouses of materials, and WWW sites. The "Selected Resources" section of this book lists some of the resources available nationally, but good external assistance may also be available within a state. For example, since 1993, a volunteer group of librarians in Michigan has operated PREMIER (Promoting Research Education in Michigan), a project of the Michigan Library Association's Information Literacy Roundtable.

This service provides a consulting group of volunteer librarians in Michigan who help campuses enhance their information literacy efforts. For example, the group offers a PREMIER self-study on research education that involves an initial meeting among PREMIER volunteers and the campus librarians, faculty, etc. After that meeting, campus personnel gather information on existing bibliographic instruction undertakings and submit them to PREMIER personnel for study so that the new efforts can build on the best efforts to date. During the second site visit, the content for a workshop is chosen, and PREMIER finds speakers and makes arrangements for a one-day colloquium that provides a focus point for accelerating faculty understanding of information literacy and moves campus planning efforts forward. During its first year of operation, PREMIER assisted Madonna College, Aquinas College, and Monroe Community College.

Another collaborative avenue for enhancing faculty involvement in information literacy efforts is to sponsor workshops that bring teams from a number of campuses together to share promising undertakings and to explore ways to enhance curriculum development efforts. A synergy consistently seems to emerge when academic officers, faculty, and librarians have time away from their campuses to consider collaborative efforts that will promote student development of strong information management and critical thinking skills. The 1995 CHE symposiums have already been highlighted, but such efforts go back to the 1970s.

In 1983, for example, a conference entitled "A Colorado Response to the Information Society: The Changing Academic Library" brought together academic vice presidents, library directors, and faculty leaders from both public and private institutions. The speakers were academic administrators and faculty who shared with those attending how they had made more than the traditional use of libraries and how, as a result, their students and campuses had benefited. The papers from this conference are still worth reading.[13] As a lasting result of this conference, the Colorado Consortium of State Colleges made enrichment funds available for a series of follow-up conferences on particular discipline areas and their relation to information and libraries.

Although a "complete" example of information literacy across the entire curriculum of a campus may not exist, an increasing number of excellent "pieces" of such programs can be found. New campus initiatives can be greatly accelerated, and dollars can be spent more wisely if campus leaders look for such models and are then willing to work collaboratively with other institutions. Moreover, the knowledge that faculty and administrators on other campuses are also working to better prepare students for lifelong learning reinforces the importance of information literacy efforts on one's own campus.

THE CHALLENGES FOR RESEARCH

Although classroom-based research has had strong proponents for many years, far less takes place than is desirable, especially in relation to information literacy initiatives.

Research Supporting Resource-Based Learning

Unfortunately, to date little research has been done to determine the impact of resource-based learning within postsecondary education. This absence of research makes the establishment of a vision and goals for programs more difficult and hinders information literacy proponents who want to champion such efforts against other undergraduate learning initiatives for limited academic attention and resources.

Although little research has been done at the postsecondary level, irrefutable research done in the K-12 setting documents how higher investments in school library media programs correlate with higher scores across the board on standardized tests.[14] This documentation includes over a decade of data from SchoolMatch, a for-profit corporation in Ohio that evaluates schools based on a database of comparative information on all public and over 12,000 accredited private schools throughout the country. According to SchoolMatch CEO William L. Bainbridge,

> Of all expenditures that influence a school's effectiveness—including those for families, teachers, guidance services and others—the levels of expenditures for library and media services have the highest correlation with student achievement.[15]

Other research documents related findings. For example, a study conducted by the Colorado State Department of Education in 1992 documents the following:

- The size of a library media center's staff and collection is the best school predictor of academic achievement. Students who score higher on norm-referenced tests tend to come from schools that have more library media staff and more books, periodicals, and videos.

- Students who score higher on norm-referenced tests tend to come from schools where the instructional role [of the library media specialist] is more prominent.[16]

Unfortunately, the K-12 research is not generally known at the school level much less at the post-secondary level. However, there is no reason to believe that what works at the K-12 level will not work a year later when the same students are in college.

Needed Research

Certainly an ideal time for researching the value-added of information literacy programs is as they are being initiated. Pilot projects that can assure the effectiveness of efforts before they are widely implemented provide an opportune time to compare student performance in the new courses with student performance in more traditional courses; or assessment of overall class research efforts can be compared with papers obtained from the semesters before and after implementation of a resource-based approach to learning. Although providing only a snapshot evaluation, such efforts can help to determine how beginning information literacy efforts can be strengthened and can provide encouragement to continue information literacy program development.

Beyond such short-term initiatives, as information literacy programs are initiated across the curriculum, consideration should be given to longer term assessment of student performance in terms of course grades, grade point average, and persistence in schooling. Certainly, the potential value of resource-based learning in meeting the individualized learning needs of highly diverse students should make such research attractive to campuses that deal with at-risk students. One controlled experiment conducted with at-risk students at Brooklyn College in 1972 supported the concept that various levels of supplemental research learning assistance could impact on student academic performance and retention.[17] Recently, the California State University System issued an RFP to benchmark student information literacy abilities on its campuses, but clearly far more research is needed in this important area.

CONCLUSION

That there are personnel and financial challenges to mounting and maintaining across-the-curriculum information literacy initiatives is clear from the experiences of campuses and from the outlook for limited increases in higher education funding. That such challenges are not insurmountable is also clear from the experiences of campuses. Where there is a conscious acknowledgment among campus leaders of the importance of students becoming information literate and where broad-based consensus building is followed by careful planning, appropriate budget and staffing realignments can and do occur to the benefit of students who will be tomorrow's Information Age leaders.

NOTES

1. Gabriela Sonntag and Donna M. Ohr, "The Development of a Lower-Division, General Education, Course-Integrated Information Literacy Program," *College & Research Libraries*, 57 (July, 1996), 334.

2. Alan E. Guskin, "The Microcomputer Revolution and the New Role of the Library: From the Perspective of a University President/Chancellor," in *A Colorado Response to the Information Society: The Changing Academic Library*, edited by Patricia Senn Breivik (Bethesda, MD: ERIC, ED 269 017, 1983), 25.

3. Lorie Roth, "Information Competence: How Close Are We?," paper presented at the Conference of the California Community Colleges, San Jose, CA, March 29, 1996.

4. Ibid.

5. Patricia Senn Breivik and J. A. Senn, *Information Literacy: Educating Children for the 21st Century* (New York: Scholastic, Inc., 1994), 83-84, citing Janadene Harvey, principal, Ernest Horn Elementary School, Iowa City, IA.

6. Wayne State University Libraries, "Information Literacy: A Student's Perspective" and "The Three Commandments for Library Instruction," January 11, 1996.

7. Robert Greenleaf. *Servant Leadership: A Journey Into the Nature of Legitimate Power and Greatness* (New York: Paulist Press, 1991).

8. Roma Harris, "Bibliographic Instruction: The Views of Academic, Special, and Public Librarians," *College & Research Libraries* (May, 1992), 255.

9. Paul T. Adalian, Jr., "CSU Information Competence Project," (San Luis Obispo, CA: California Polytechnic State University, Robert E. Kennedy Library, 1997); accessed January 27, 1997 at http://www.lib.calpoly.edu./infocomp/index.html.

10. Taken from information submitted by the University of Maryland Eastern Shore in response to a 1994/1995 survey regarding information literacy programs conducted by the Commission on Higher Education of the Middle States Association of Colleges and Schools, the Western Association of Schools and Colleges, and the Association of College and Research Libraries.

11. Ibid.

12. Christine Bruce, (1994) Griffith University Information Literacy Blueprint in *The Learning Link, Information Literacy in Practice*, edited by Di Booker, (Adelaide, Australia: AUSLIB PRESS, 1995).

13. Patricia Senn Breivik, ed., *A Colorado Response to the Information Society: The Changing Academic Library* (Bethesda, MD: ERIC, Ed 269 017, 1983).

14. Patricia Senn Breivik and J. A. Senn, *Information Literacy: Educating Children for the 21st Century*, rev. ed. (Washington, DC: NEA, 1997), 188.

15. William L. Bainbridge, "Morning Edition," radio talk show *National Public Radio*, January 13, 1987.

16. Colorado Department of Education, *Highlights from the Impact of School Library Media Centers on Academic Achievements* (Denver: Colorado Department of Education, September 1992), 96.
17. Patricia Senn Breivik, *Open Admissions and the Academic Library* (Chicago: American Library Association, 1977), 57-59.

CHAPTER 7

Moving Forward

People who are information literate—who know how to acquire knowledge and use it—are America's most valuable resource.
— ALA Presidential Committee on Information Literacy:
Final Report, 1989

A striking television ad for an automobile pictures boats floating down the water-filled streets of a major city. One car drives purposefully around the ships and boats while a voice asks, "Why float through life when you can drive?" Such a question challenges campuses today—will they equip their students to move deliberately, wisely, and effectively though today's Information Society, or will students be left to coast through life largely at the mercy of the prevailing winds of the popular media and the currents of popular sentiment?

Growing numbers of academicians are making serious commitments to empowering their students for lifelong learning and quality lives in this Information Age. Given that the Final Report of the American Library Association Presidential Committee on Information Literacy was only released in 1989, the amount of thoughtful activity directed toward the achievement of such empowerment is remarkable, particularly since the education reform reports of the 1980s had overlooked such concerns. Nor does this growth in activity seem to be slowing. For example, the Commission on Higher Education (CHE) of the Middle States Association of Colleges and Schools documented a 15 percent increase in the number of campuses in its region sponsoring information literacy programs between fall 1994 and fall 1995.[1] How can such progress be explained?

First, the time was and is right. Rapidly changing information technology is beginning to permeate people's daily lives, and the Clinton-Gore administration has placed great importance on making technology a part of the solution to the education and economic development challenges facing this country. At the same time, the criticisms raised in the reform reports are not being well addressed, and complaints primarily from the business sector have kept pressure on schools and colleges to produce students who can think critically, solve problems, and communicate effectively. Finally, many campuses have well-established library bibliographic/instruction programs that are the result of efforts by some faculty and librarians who understand that just teaching today's facts is not enough to prepare students for effective careers or quality lives in an information society.

Other factors explain this progress, of course, but these three streams of activity are the primary force behind the receptive and action-oriented responses to the 1989 information literacy report and the challenges issued by such leaders as James B. Appleberry, E. Gordon Gee, Alan E. Guskin, Howard Simmons, and Ralph Wolff. The National Forum for Information Literacy has also played a valuable role in connecting information literacy to the mission of a widely divergent group of national organizations.

Conceptually, if not in actuality, all of higher education has crossed the Rubicon. There is no turning back. It is simply no longer possible to equate a quality education with only the mastery of currently accepted facts, because information is expanding far too quickly. Instead, students must be prepared for learning throughout their lifetimes and in all facets of their lives. Nothing can change that reality, and academic programs across the country will sooner or later have to adjust their curriculums to accommodate this reality.

If you believe it is time for your campus to move ahead, what can you do— as a faculty member, librarian, department chair, dean, academic vice president or president—to move forward information literacy planning on your campus? You can start today to follow five practical steps.

MAKE A COMMITMENT

The logical place to start is with yourself. As an academic leader, take the time to think through how the concept of information literacy relates to your campus and its departmental mission statements and goals, and how the concept relates to existing academic priorities on campus. Because only so many challenges can be addressed at one time, information literacy has to become one of the "must be's" on your list of priorities. Are you willing to begin the shift away from the lecture-textbook-reserves delivery style to learning— regardless of any initial resistance? Are you personally ready to make a commitment to information literacy?

If you are not yet certain, then you need to learn more about information literacy. Check the websites listed in the "Selected Resources" section of this book. Call people whose current information literacy efforts, as described in this book, particularly interest you; talk to them about what they are doing and what pay-offs they and their students are experiencing. Better still, if possible, visit their campuses so you can see resource-based learning in action and talk firsthand with those who are involved.

If, however, you are convinced that information literacy is essential to a quality education for all students on your campus, then the next logical step is to develop a plan.

DEVELOP A PLAN

Although a single faculty member or librarian can make small changes that will begin to produce some information-literate students, any sweeping campus changes will come only as a result of a broad academic plan for the college or university. The plan will include a systematic consideration of how to integrate information resources and technology into the curriculum so that students will have the opportunity to become effective lifelong learners.

Begin by Asking Questions

Because colleges and universities are complex institutions—each with its own individual mission and environment—each plan will ultimately be unique in some ways. One of the best ways, therefore, to begin developing the plan for your campus is to target key individuals and groups and ask them lots of vital questions. For example, in 1983, Towson University President Hoke Smith called for the establishment of a faculty committee "to evaluate our resources, to study the opportunities and threats which [the move toward a knowledge-based society] creates, to make initial recommendations to the appropriate university governing bodies, and to propose a permanent governance structure to assist in providing leadership in determining ways of relating to and using the electronic technological environment which is now developing as the basis of the Information Age."[2]

President Smith's challenge was driven by his belief that the curriculum needed to change if it was to successfully prepare students for lives and careers in the Information Age. He wanted to initiate discussions among faculty on how Towson University should relate to the role of information in society, how it should explore or take advantage of the fact that information has economic value, and, most important, how it should reflect these issues within its academic programs. It took many years of asking, but, by continuing to rephrase and refocus this question, progress was made. Today, Towson University is an exemplary model for integrating information resources and technology into general education offerings.

Hoke Smith is not alone. Among other campus leaders who are developing a vision by first asking questions is Blenda J. Wilson, president of California State University, Northridge.

> "To a man with a hammer, everything looks like a nail." To a man with a computer, everything looks like—what?—data, instead of thought; calculation, instead of judgement; ubiquitous access, instead of judicious choice; speed, instead of introspection; individual omniscience, instead of social interdependence? What? We need to think about that. . . . Higher education faces many daunting challenges. The tools that computers and advanced technology represent can be of extraordinary value in meeting those challenges if they are designed to serve our noble mission. I believe that can happen only if we take responsibility for what we allow it to do and also for what we allow it to undo.[3]

Questions like these, when asked and reasked in ways that are meaningful to different campus constituencies, can and will produce campus dialogues that will eventually lead to both a shared vision among, at least, a leadership group and a plan for how to reach that vision.

Provide a Common Vocabulary

Before the vision can be promoted widely on a campus, it must have a common vocabulary. Some campuses prefer to discuss *information competencies* instead of *information literacy*. Another frequently used term in the medical and health sciences is *informatics*. Resource-based learning may also be called *inquiry learning* or *undergraduate research*. Always keep in mind, however, that the terminology you use is not as important as having a shared vocabulary and a clear understanding of what is meant by the adopted terminology.

SELL THE VISION

After the vision is firmly established, the next logical step is to share that vision with others on campus and give them opportunities to see resource-based learning in action. Highlight your best campus examples and share a few carefully selected articles with faculty. (Match the articles to specific discipline models whenever possible.) Make sure the appropriate faculty committees are exploring information literacy and resource-based learning from the perspective of their charges—whether that is campus technology or student retention.

Eventually the vision will also have to be sold to students. However, when the faculty are firmly committed to the vision, their course syllabi will reflect that commitment. The second "sell" will then take care of itself.

CONDUCT A CAMPUS AUDIT

As part of a committed focus on information literacy, campus leaders need to conduct a systematic audit of existing incentives and disincentives to the involvement of faculty and librarians in pursuing a resource-based learning approach to teaching/learning. In particular, this is the time to examine promotion and tenure criteria, faculty and staff development opportunities, and curricular requirements. It is also the time to see the establishment of specific acknowledgments and awards for those whose efforts are noteworthy.

Part of this campus audit should also include consideration of existing campus resources that are positioned or can be redeployed to support information literacy across the curriculum. What is the quality of the learning resources on campus and what opportunities to access off-campus resources exist? Is there a sufficient range of formats to accommodate differences in learning styles? Do students, as well as faculty, have adequate access to technology for research and learning? Are there physical spaces in the library and other appropriate places to facilitate team projects and other interaction among students, faculty, and librarians? Insofar as weaknesses are discovered, establish a plan for addressing them.

MEASURE AND CELEBRATE SUCCESSES

As programs are established, take time to create measurements of success. Ideally, both short- and longer-term results should be measured. Quality of student research and quality of the presentations of student findings can be evaluated for immediate feedback on the effectiveness of new resource-based learning efforts, and alumni surveys can provide insights into on-the-job impact of information literacy programs. But the primary value of your assessment efforts will be the early detection and redirection of any learning effort that is not producing the intended outcomes in students' mastery of information literacy abilities; and, where assessments of student performance indicate success, these results can be used to encourage buy-in by other faculty to the value of information literacy programs.

Indeed, when there are successes—and there will be successes—celebrate them! One of the most powerful tools you have to promote information literacy on any campus is simply letting people know when and where good results are being achieved. From the student newspaper, to the institution's annual report, and at every possible public occasion, let people know how students are being empowered for academic success and lifelong learning.

CONCLUSION

Ten or 15 years ago busy academic leaders may have been excused for ignoring questions about how the Information Age would affect the curriculum. The recent and ongoing explosion of information, however, has entirely changed the landscape forever. Now the bottom line for academic leaders is this: *When will this campus embrace information literacy programs?* No longer is there a choice because the stakes are higher than they have ever been before. If no changes are made, the very quality of life for all future generations will be in jeopardy. The majority of graduates who are not information literate will *not* be able to "drive" through the rest of their lives with confidence—in control of where they are going—because they will be drowning in a sea of information when making personal, business, and civic decisions.

Everyone in higher education today can and must make a difference in the future by moving each and every campus toward resource-based learning with the goal of graduating information-literate, lifelong learners. These graduates will become future teachers, politicians, judges, doctors, and parents—the Information Age leaders of the United States. What a challenge! And what a privilege to be part of that calling!

NOTES

1. Commission on Higher Education of the Middle States Association of Colleges and Schools, *1996 and Beyond* (Philadelphia: Commission on Higher Education, 1996), 27.
2. Patricia Senn Breivik, "Investing Wisely in Information Technology: Asking the Right Questions," *Educational Record*, 74 (Summer 1993), 47-48, as cited in Hoke L. Smith, "The State of the University: An Address to the Faculty," Towson State University, September 15, 1983, 10.
3. Blenda J. Wilson, "Technology and Higher Education: In Search of Progress in Human Learning," *Educational Record*, 75 (Summer 1994), 15-16.

POSTSCRIPT FOR EARLY LEADERS

Better education in how to use information is an essential component of rational public policy toward the information sector.

—Roger G. Noll

Those who are already in the trenches fighting to promote information literacy—those who bought this book to give to someone else—your leadership is needed to meet several further challenges. The twenty-first century is here in all practical terms, and, it is regretable that most of higher education is still not well positioned to graduate students who will feel secure as they set off down the information superhighway; nor will they be able to adapt and function confidently in the twists and turns the superhighway is bound to take throughout their lives. To reach the goal of information literacy for all students, three largely unexplored issues on campuses and an even greater issue beyond campus boundaries must be addressed. These four major challenges require the attention of the makers and shapers of today's and tomorrow's Information Age graduates.

ENSURING CHANGES IN TEACHER EDUCATION

Particular attention must be paid to the state of affairs in colleges of education. Until resource-based learning permeates the curriculum in the programs that prepare future teachers, the classrooms of our nation's schools will continue to fall short of meeting the individual learning needs of students and of preparing students to be lifelong learners. In an article coauthored with Dennis Hinkle, dean of the College of Education at Towson University (TU), I describe the initial steps taken at the TU College of Education to fulfill its theme of being "The college that prepares teachers as facilitators of active learning," as well as to challenge other teacher educators to be leaders on their own campuses.

As professional educators, faculty in colleges of education can serve as effective models for demonstrating resource-based learning. Who better to provide models than education faculty who understand and propagate the learning process? Is this not the group that should take the lead on campus in collaborative curriculum planning with librarians and media specialists? Is this not the group to serve as models not only for beginning teacher candidates, but also for experienced teachers and other campus faculty?[1]

Unfortunately, few colleges of education seem to share such concerns, since there was little response to a brief questionnaire regarding the state of information literacy in teacher education programs that appeared in the same issue of *AACTE Briefs* as the above article. Clearly, campus information literacy leaders need to target their colleges of education for loving attention!

However, given the number of years it will take before enough information-literate teachers are graduated, academic leaders should also build upon existing partnerships or establish new ones with schools in their communities to a promote resource-based learning. One good example of such efforts, which is concerned with resource-based learning, is the National Education Association's Teacher Education Initiative (TEI). This collaborative effort with selected P-12 schools and colleges of education across the nation considers resource-based learning within its commitment to transform "teaching and learning to meet the present and future needs of students" and also "to function as a unifying element to guide, support, and facilitate significant improvement in teacher preparation programs."[2]

COLLABORATION WITH STUDENT SERVICES

Academic partnerships with student services should be formed to seek opportunities for students at all levels to experience the importance of information literacy outside as well as inside the classroom. Some research already exists on the importance of this broader perspective on student learning in regard to students' development of critical thinking skills such as is reflected in the following quote from a paper presented at the 1993 meeting of the Association for Institutional Research:

Institutional and academic program planning processes, these findings suggest, are more likely to be successful and effective if they take into account the potential for simultaneous contributions of students' class-related and out-of-class experiences on student learning. Gains in critical thinking appear to be a consequence of a variety of student experiences, not just those that are part of the formal instructional program. Ways must be found to overcome the artificial, organizational bifurcation of our education delivery systems. Academic and student affairs units have common goals, and the evidence of this study suggests that students are more likely to benefit educationally if these units work together, rather than separately, in pursuit of those common goals.[3]

Lois M. Stanford, vice president of student and academic services at the University of Alberta, suggests that there "are two areas in which the information literacy philosophy of education could match with goals of student services. These [are] recruitment and retention of the excellent student, and retention and success with the at-risk student."[4] She further suggests that to outstanding students "an education based explicitly on skills for the twenty-first century might be powerfully attractive bait. And what skills would one advertise? Information literacy for an information society."[5] She also suggests that classroom and library instructors need to take joint responsibility for providing at-risk students with the information literacy learning experiences they need to "responsibly and productively" use the world of microcomputers and the campus information network, and for providing first-year courses that are focused on information literacy and a resource-based learning methodology.

PURSUING NEEDED RESEARCH AND SERVICE

The Information Age, with all its associated problems and opportunities, is still in its infancy. So much is still unknown about its implications for the present and the future. Besides assessment of the outcomes of campus information literacy programs, efforts need to be directed toward such topics as the information needs of different community groups, the impact of information literacy on work force productivity and the quality of people's lives, and the impact of resource-based learning on students' academic success—to name just a few.

In addition, within the service commitment of campuses a different more hands-on type of information literacy research can be accomplished. For example, faculty can become involved in community-based efforts to improve schools, such as those sponsored by the National Association of Partners in Education, or can initiate efforts to bring K-12, higher education, parents, and business groups together for such purposes.

ASKING THE RIGHT QUESTIONS

Finally, your leadership is required for a pressing need beyond the education sector. Beyond asking the right questions on your own campus about wise investments in technology and empowering people to use information resources and technology effectively, similar questions need to be addressed to people at all levels of government and across the business sector.

Higher education, which has always been the leading producer of information and whose libraries have been the leading organizers of information for use by scholars and students, is desperately needed to play a leadership role beyond its campuses in regard to information policy setting and management. It must not allow public policy to further the gap between the haves and the have-nots in society. It must not let state or national leaders believe that any technology is *the* answer or that hooking schools to the Internet will in and of itself improve student learning. Among other things, higher education must champion the role of public libraries in ensuring people's right to intellectual participation. This new challenge to the democratic way of life in the United States is well captured in the 1994 comments of Peter Young, executive director of the U.S. National Commission on Libraries and Information Science.

> We are approaching a sea change in history, where the public's right to equal access to the tools required to navigate successfully in the global infosphere of the twenty-first century requires a rebalancing and rearticulation in order to assure that democratic principles and basic, humanistic values continue to function as the presuppositions of our society and that these same values and principles are reflected in the information infrastructure available to all Americans.[6]

Anne Wells Branscomb, scholar in residence at the Annenberg Public Policy Center of the University of Pennsylvania, also addressed this critical need in a 1994 speech.

> With the explosion of information, the expansion of electronic highways and the increase of knowledge generally, there should be no information poor. Our information environment can be enriched for everyone, if we deploy the hardware and software wisely within a legal structure which is fair and just.[7]

Even when information is readily available, the people who need it most might not be able to use it. Research on issues such as the "Knowledge Gap, Information-Seeking and the Poor" deserves far greater attention. A 1995 article summarized some of the research done to date and concluded that

> If disadvantaged members of a social environment experience gaps, perhaps it is gaps in second-level knowledge, or knowledge about which they do not know; nor does anyone else know. . . . This is knowledge that originates outside of lived experiences. Because it addressed things we have not previously experienced, its relevance to our specific circumstances is questionable. Verification of its truthfulness is also problematic. So, even if the poor are exposed to a wide

variety of information, they might not accept these sources as ways in which to better their situations.[8]

Hopes, therefore, of purely technological solutions to people's information needs are shortsighted. Community-based, people-friendly public librarians will far better meet the needs of many people than self-service information kiosks ever will. Who better than academic leaders to influence other decision makers to make wise investments in technology and to create sound public policy in regards to information dissemination and use? And who better than you?

NOTES

Epigraph: Roger G. Noll, "The Economics of Information: A User's Guide," *The Annual Review* (1993-94).

1. Patricia Senn Breivik and Dennis Hinkle, "Information Literacy: Educating Teachers for the 21st Century," *AACTE Briefs*, 17 (April 22, 1996), 6-7.

2. "Teacher Education Initiative," National Education Association paper, September 11, 1995.

3. Patrick T. Terenzini, Leonard Springer, Ernest T. Pascarella, and Amaury Nora, "Influences Affecting the Development of Students' Critical Thinking Skills," *Research in Higher Education*, 36, No. 1 (1995), 36.

4. Lois M. Stanford, "An Academician's Journey Into Information Literacy," *Information Literacy: Developing Students as Independent Learners, New Directions for Higher Education*, No. 78, edited by D. W. Farmer and Terrence F. Mech (San Francisco: Jossey-Bass Publishers, Summer 1992), 41.

5. Ibid.

6. Peter Young, "Changing Information Access Economics: New Roles for Libraries and Librarians," *Information Technology and Libraries*, 13 (June, 1994), 114.

7. Anne Wells Branscomb, "Public and Private Domains of Information: Defining the Legal Boundaries," *Bulletin of the American Society for Information Science*, 23 (December/January, 1995), 18.

8. Elfreda A. Chatman and Victoria E.M. Pendelton, "Knowledge Gap, Information-Seeking and the Poor," *The Reference Librarian*, Nos. 49/50, (1995), 143.

APPENDIX A

Final Report of the American Library Association Presidential Committee on Information Literacy

No other change in American society has offered greater challenges than the emergence of the Information Age. Information is expanding at an unprecedented rate, and enormously rapid strides are being made in the technology for storing, organizing, and accessing the ever growing tidal wave of information. The combined effect of these factors is an increasingly fragmented information base—large components of which are only available to people with money and/or acceptable institutional affiliations.

Yet in an information society all people should have the right to information which can enhance their lives. Out of the super-abundance of available information, people need to be able to obtain specific information to meet a wide range of personal and business needs. These needs are largely driven either by the desire for personal growth and advancement or by the rapidly changing social, political, and economic environments of American society. What is true today is often outdated tomorrow. A good job today may be obsolete next year. To promote economic independence and quality of existence, there is a lifelong need for being informed and up-to-date.

How our country deals with the realities of the Information Age will have enormous impact on our democratic way of life and on our nation's ability to compete internationally. Within America's information society, there also exists the potential of addressing many long-standing social and economic inequities. To reap such benefits, people—as individuals and as a nation—must be information literate. To be information literate, a person must be able to recognize when information is needed and have the ability to locate, evaluate, and use effectively the needed information. Producing such a citizenry will require that schools and colleges appreciate and integrate the concept of information literacy into their learning programs and that they play a leadership role in equipping individuals and institutions to take advantage of the opportunities inherent within the information society. Ultimately, information literate people are those who have learned how to learn. They know how to learn because they know how knowledge is organized, how to find information, and how to use information in such a way that others can learn from them. They are people prepared for lifelong learning, because they can always find the information needed for any task or decision at hand.

THE IMPORTANCE OF INFORMATION LITERACY TO INDIVIDUALS, BUSINESS, AND CITIZENSHIP

In Individuals' Lives

Americans have traditionally valued quality of life and the pursuit of happiness; however, these goals are increasingly difficult to achieve because of the complexities of life in today's information and technology dependent society. The cultural and educational opportunities available in an average community, for example, are often missed by people who lack the ability to keep informed of such activities, and lives of information illiterates are more likely than others to be narrowly focused on second-hand experiences of life through television. On the other hand, life is more interesting when one knows what is going on, what opportunities exist, and where alternatives to current practices can be discovered.

On a daily basis, problems are more difficult to solve when people lack access to meaningful information vital to good decision making. Many people are vulnerable to poorly informed people or opportunists when selecting nursing care for a parent or facing a major expense such as purchasing, financing, or insuring a new home or car. Other information-dependent decisions can affect one's entire lifetime. For example, what information do young people have available to them when they consider which college to attend or whether to become sexually active? Even in areas where one can achieve an expertise, constantly changing and expanding information bases necessitate an ongoing struggle for individuals to keep up-to-date and in control of their daily information environment as well as with information from other fields which can affect the outcomes of their decisions.

In an attempt to reduce information to easily manageable segments, most people have become dependent on others for their information. Information prepackaging in schools and through broadcast and print news media, in fact, encourages people to accept the opinions of others without much thought. When opinions are biased, negative, or inadequate for the needs at hand, many people are left helpless to improve the situation confronting them. Imagine, for example, a family which is being evicted by a landlord who claims he is within his legal rights. Usually they will have to accept the landlord's "expert" opinion, because they do not know how to seek information to confirm or disprove his claim. Information literacy, therefore, is a means of personal empowerment. It allows people to verify or refute expert opinion and to become independent seekers of truth. It provides them with the ability to build their own arguments and to experience the excitement of the search for knowledge. It not only prepares them for lifelong learning; but, by experiencing the excitement of their own successful quests for knowledge, it also creates in young people the motivation for pursuing learning throughout their lives.

Moreover, the process of searching and interacting with the ideas and values of their own and others' cultures deepens people's capacities to understand and position themselves within larger communities of time and place. By drawing on the arts, history, and literature of previous generations, individuals and communities can affirm the best in their cultures and determine future goals.

It is unfortunate that the very people who most need the empowerment inherent in being information literate are the least likely to have learning experiences which will promote these abilities. Minority and at-risk students, illiterate adults, people with English as a second language, and economically disadvantaged people are among those most likely to lack access to the information that can improve their situations. Most are not even aware of the potential help that is available to them. Libraries, which provide the best access point to information for most U.S. citizens, are left untapped by those who most need help to improve their quality of life. As former U.S. Secretary of Education Terrell Bell once wrote, "There is a danger of a new elite developing in our country: the information elite."[1]

In Business

Herbert E. Meyer, who has served as an editor for *Fortune* magazine and as vice-chairman of the National Intelligence Council, underscores the importance of access to and use of good information for business in an age characterized by rapid change, a global environment, and unprecedented access to information. In his 1988 book, *Real World Intelligence*,[2] he describes the astonishment and growing distress of executives who "are discovering that the only thing as difficult and dangerous as managing a large enterprise with too little information is managing one with too much" (p.29). While Meyer emphasizes that companies should rely on public sources that are available to anyone for much of their information (p. 36), it is clear that many companies do not know how to find and use such information effectively. Every day lack of timely and accurate information is costly to American businesses. The following examples document cases of such losses or near losses.

A manufacturing company had a research team of three scientists and four technicians working on a project, and at the end of a year the team felt it had a patentable invention in addition to a new product. Prior to filing the patent application, the company's patent attorney requested a literature search. While doing the search, the librarian found that the proposed application duplicated some of the work claimed in a patent that had been issued about a year before the team had begun its work. During the course of the project the company had spent almost $500,000 on the project, an outlay that could have been avoided if it had spent the approximately $300 required to have a review of the literature completed before beginning the project.

A manufacturing company was sued by an individual who claimed that the company had stolen his "secret formula" for a product that the company had just marketed. An information scientist on the staff of the company's technical library found a reference in the technical literature that this formula was generally known to the trade long before the litigant developed his "secret formula." When he was presented with this information, the litigant dropped his $7 million claim.

When the technical librarian for an electronics firm was asked to do a literature search for one of its engineers, four people had already been working to resolve a problem for more than a year. The literature search found an article that contained the answer the engineer needed to solve his problem. The article had been published several years before the project team had begun its work. Had the literature search been conducted when the problem was first identified, the company could have saved four man-years of labor and its resulting direct monetary costs.[3]

The need for people in business who are competent managers of information is important at all levels, and the realities of the Information Age require serious rethinking of how businesses should be conducted. Harlan Cleveland explores this theme in his book, *The Knowledge Executive*. Information (organized data, the raw material for specialized knowledge, and generalist wisdom) is now our most important, and pervasive resource. Information workers now compose more than half the U.S. labor force. But this newly dominant resource is quite unlike the tangible resources we have heretofore thought of as valuable. The differences help explain why we get into so much trouble trying to use for the management of information concepts that worked all right in understanding the management of things—concepts such as control, secrecy, ownership, privilege and geopolitics. Because the old pyramids of influence and control were based on just these ideas, they are now crumbling. Their weakening is not always obvious, just as a wooden structure may look solid when you can't see what termites have done to its insides. Whether this "crumble effect" will result in a fairer shake for the world's disadvantaged majority is not yet clear. But there is ample evidence that those who learn how to achieve access to the bath of knowledge that already envelops the world will be the future's aristocrats of achievement, and that they will be far more numerous than any aristocracy in history.[4]

In Citizenship

American democracy has led to the evolution of many thousands of organized citizen groups that seek to influence public policy, issues, and community problems. Following are just a few examples.

A local League of Women Voters has been chosen to study housing patterns for low-income individuals in its community. It must inform its members of the options for low-income housing and, in the process, comment publicly on the city's long-range, low-income housing plans.

In an upper Midwestern city, one with the highest unemployment rate in 50 years, a major automobile company offers to build a new assembly plant in the central city. The only stipulation is that the city condemn property in a poor ethnic neighborhood of 3,500 residents for use as the site of its plant. In addition, the company seeks a twelve year tax abatement. Residents of the neighborhood frantically seek to find out how they might save their community from the wrecker's ball but still improve their tax base.

A group of upper-middle-class women in the Junior League has read about increased incidences of child abuse. They want to become better informed about the elements of child abuse: What brings it on? What incidents have occurred in their own community? What services are available in their community? What actions might they take?[5]

To address these problems successfully, each of these groups will have to secure access to a wide range of information, much of which—if they know how to find it—can be obtained without any cost to their organizations. Citizenship in a modern democracy involves more than knowledge of how to access vital information. It also involves a capacity to recognize propaganda, distortion, and other misuses and abuses of information. People are daily subjected to statistics about health, the economy, national defense, and countless products. One person arranges the information to prove his point, another arranges it to prove hers. One political party says the social indicators are encouraging, another calls them frightening. One drug company states most doctors prefer its product, another "proves" doctors favor its product. In such an environment, information literacy provides insight into the manifold ways in which people can all be deceived and misled. Information literate citizens are able to spot and expose chicanery, disinformation, and lies.

To say that information literacy is crucial to effective citizenship is simply to say it is central to the practice of democracy. Any society committed to individual freedom and democratic government must ensure the free flow of information to all its citizens in order to protect personal liberties and to guard its future. As U.S. Representative Major R. Owens has said:

> Information literacy is needed to guarantee the survival of democratic institutions. All men are created equal but voters with information resources are in a position to make more intelligent decisions than citizens who are information illiterates. The application of information resources to the process of decision-making to fulfill civic responsibilities is a vital necessity.[6]

OPPORTUNITIES TO DEVELOP INFORMATION LITERACY

Information literacy is a survival skill in the Information Age. Instead of drowning in the abundance of information that floods their lives, information literate people know how to find, evaluate, and use information effectively to solve a particular problem or make a decision—whether the information they select comes from a computer, a book, a government agency, a film, or any number of other possible resources. Libraries, which provide a significant public access point to such information and usually at no cost, must play a key role in preparing people for the demands of today's information society. Just as public libraries were once a means of education and a better life for many of the over 20 million immigrants of the late 1800s and early 1900s, they remain today as the potentially strongest and most far-reaching community resource for lifelong learning. Public libraries not only provide access to information, but they also remain crucial to providing people with the knowledge necessary to make meaningful use of existing resources. They remain one of the few safeguards against information control by a minority.

Although libraries historically have provided a meaningful structure for relating information in ways that facilitate the development of knowledge, they have been all but ignored in the literature about the information society. Even national education reform reports, starting with A Nation at Risk[7] in 1983, largely exclude libraries. No K-12 report has explored the potential role of libraries or the need for information literacy. In the higher education reform literature, Education Commission of the States President Frank Newman's 1985 report, Higher Education and the American Resurgence,[8] only addresses the instructional potential of libraries in passing, but it does raise the concern for the accessibility of materials within the knowledge explosion. In fact, no reform report until College,[9] the 1986 Carnegie Foundation Report, gave substantive consideration to the role of libraries in addressing the challenges facing higher education. In the initial release of the study's recommendations, it was noted that

The quality of a college is measured by the resources for learning on the campus and the extent to which students become independent, self-directed learners. And yet we found that today, about one out of every four undergraduates spends no time in the library during a normal week, and 65 percent use the library four hours or less each week. The gap between the classroom and the library, reported on almost a half-century ago, still exists today.[10]

Statistics such as these document the general passivity of most academic learning today and the divorce of the impact of the Information Age from prevailing teaching styles.

The first step in reducing this gap is making sure that the issue of information literacy is an integral part of current efforts at cultural literacy, the development of critical thinking abilities, and school restructuring. Due to the relative newness of the information society, however, information literacy is often completely overlooked in relevant dialogues, research, and experimentations. Moreover, most current educational and communication endeavors—with their long-standing history of pre-packaging information—militate against the development of even an awareness of the need to master information management skills.

The effects of such prepackaging of information are most obvious in the school and academic settings. Students, for example, receive predigested information from lectures and textbooks, and little in their environment fosters active thinking or problem solving. What problem solving does occur is within artificially constructed and limited information environments that allow for single "correct" answers. Such exercises bear little resemblance to problem solving in the real world where multiple solutions of varying degrees of usefulness must be pieced together—often from many disciplines and from multiple information sources such as online databases, videotapes, government documents, and journals.

Education needs a new model of learning—learning that is based on the information resources of the real world and learning that is active and integrated, not passive and fragmented. On an intellectual level, many teachers and school administrators recognize that lectures, textbooks, materials put on reserve, and tests that ask students to regurgitate data from these sources do not create an active, much less a quality, learning experience. Moreover, studies at the higher education level have proven that students fail to retain most information they are "given."

The curve for forgetting course content is fairly steep: a generous estimate is that students forget 50% of the content within a few months. . . . A more devastating finding comes from a study that concluded that even under the most favorable conditions, "students carry away in their heads and in their notebooks not more than 42% of the lecture content." Those were the results when students were told that they would be tested immediately following the lecture; they were permitted to use their notes; and they were given a prepared summary of the lecture. These results were bad enough, but when students were tested a week later, without the use of their notes, they could recall only 17% of the lecture material.[11]

Because of the rapidly shrinking half-life of information, even the value of that 17% that students do remember must be questioned. To any thoughtful person, it must be clear that teaching facts is a poor substitute for teaching people how to learn, i.e., giving them the skills to be able to locate, evaluate, and effectively use information for any given need. What is called for is not a new information studies curriculum but, rather, a restructuring of the learning process. Textbooks, workbooks, and lectures must yield to a learning process based on the information resources available for learning and problem solving throughout people's lifetimes—to learning experiences that build a lifelong habit of library use. Such a learning process would actively involve students in the process of

- knowing when they have a need for information
- identifying information needed to address a given problem or issue
- finding needed information and evaluating the information
- organizing the information
- using the information effectively to address the problem or issue at hand.

Such a restructuring of the learning process will not only enhance the critical thinking skills of students but will also empower them for lifelong learning and the effective performance of professional and civic responsibilities.

AN INFORMATION AGE SCHOOL

An increased emphasis on information literacy and resource-based learning would manifest itself in a variety of ways at both the academic and school levels, depending upon the role and mission of the individual institution and the information environment of its community. However, the following description of what a school might be like if information literacy were a central, not a peripheral, concern reveals some of the possibilities. (While focused on K-12, outcomes could be quite similar at the college level.)

The school would be more interactive, because students, pursuing questions of personal interest, would be interacting with other students, with teachers, with a vast array of information resources, and the community at large to a far greater degree than they presently do today. One would expect to find every student engaged in at least one open-ended, long-term quest for an answer to a serious social, scientific, aesthetic, or political problem. Students' quests would involve not only searching print, electronic, and video data, but also interviewing people inside and outside of school. As a result, learning would be more self-initiated. There would be more reading of original sources and more extended writing. Both students and teachers would be familiar with the intellectual and emotional demands of asking productive questions, gathering data of all kinds, reducing and synthesizing information, and analyzing, interpreting, and evaluating information in all its forms. In such an environment, teachers would be coaching and guiding students more and lecturing less. They would have long since discovered that the classroom computer, with its access to the libraries and databases of the world, is a better source of facts than they could ever hope to be. They would have come to see that their major importance lies in their capacity to arouse curiosity and guide it to a satisfactory conclusion, to ask the right questions at the right time, to stir debate and serious discussion, and to be models themselves of thoughtful inquiry.

Teachers would work consistently with librarians, media resource people, and instructional designers both within their schools and in their communities to ensure that student projects and explorations are challenging, interesting, and productive learning experiences in which they can all take pride. It would not be surprising in such a school to find a student task force exploring an important community issue with a view toward making a public presentation of its findings on cable television or at a news conference. Nor would it be unusual to see the librarian guiding the task force through its initial questions and its multi-disciplinary, multimedia search all the way through to its cable or satellite presentation. In such a role, librarians would be valued for their information expertise and their technological know-how. They would lead frequent in-service teacher workshops and ensure that the school was getting the most out of its investment in information technology.

Because evaluation in such a school would also be far more interactive than it is today, it would also be a much better learning experience. Interactive tutoring software that guides students through their own and other knowledge bases would provide more useful diagnostic information than is available today. Evaluation would be based upon a broad range of literacy indicators, including some that assess the quality and appropriateness of information sources or the quality and efficiency of the information searches themselves. Assessments would attend to ways in which students are using their minds and achieving success as information consumers, analyzers, interpreters, evaluators, and communicators of ideas.

Finally, one would expect such a school to look and sound different from today's schools. One would see more information technology than is evident today, and it would be important to people not only in itself but also in regard to its capacity to help them solve problems and create knowledge. One would see the fruits of many student projects prominently displayed on the walls and on bookshelves, and one would hear more discussions and debate about substantive, relevant issues. On the playground, in the halls, in the cafeteria, and certainly in the classroom, one would hear fundamental questions that make information literacy so important: "How do you know that?" and "What evidence do you have for that?" "Who says?" and "How can we find out?"

CONCLUSION

This call for more attention to information literacy comes at a time when many other learning deficiencies are being expressed by educators, business leaders, and parents. Many workers, for example, appear unprepared to deal effectively with the challenges of high-tech equipment. There exists a need for better thinkers, problem solvers, and inquirers. There are calls for computer literacy, civic literacy, global literacy, and cultural literacy. Because we have been hit by a tidal wave of information, what used to suffice as literacy no longer suffices; what used to count as effective knowledge no longer meets our needs; what used to pass as a good education no longer is adequate.

The one common ingredient in all of these concerns is an awareness of the rapidly changing requirements for a productive, healthy, and satisfying life. To respond effectively to an ever-changing environment, people need more than just a knowledge base, they also need techniques for exploring it, connecting it to other knowledge bases, and making practical use of it. In other words, the landscape upon which we used to stand has been transformed, and we are being forced to establish a new foundation called information literacy. Now knowledge—not minerals or agricultural products or manufactured goods—is this country's most precious commodity, and people who are information literate—who know how to acquire knowledge and use it—are America's most valuable resources.

COMMITTEE RECOMMENDATIONS

To reap the benefits from the Information Age by our country, its citizens, and its businesses, the American Library Association Presidential Committee on Information Literacy makes the following recommendations:

1. We all must reconsider the ways we have organized information institutionally, structured information access, and defined information's role in our lives at home, in the community, and in the work place. To the extent that our concepts about knowledge and information are out of touch with the realities of a new, dynamic information environment, we

must reconceptualize them. The degrees and directions of reconceptualization will vary, but the aims should always be the same: to communicate the power of knowledge; to develop in each citizen a sense of his or her responsibility to acquire knowledge and deepen insight through better use of information and related technologies; to instill a love of learning, a thrill in searching, and a joy in discovering; and to teach young and old alike how to know when they have an information need and how to gather, synthesize, analyze, interpret, and evaluate the information around them. All of these abilities are equally important for the enhancement of life experiences and for business pursuits. Colleges, schools, and businesses should pay special attention to the potential role of their libraries or information centers. These should be central, not peripheral; organizational redesigns should seek to empower students and adults through new kinds of access to information and new ways of creating, discovering, and sharing it.

2. A Coalition for Information Literacy should be formed under the leadership of the American Library Association, in coordination with other national organizations and agencies, to promote information literacy. The major obstacle to promoting information literacy is a lack of public awareness of the problems created by information illiteracy. The need for increased information literacy levels in all aspects of people's lives—in business, in family matters, and civic responsibilities—must be brought to the public's attention in a forceful way. To accomplish this, the Coalition should serve as an educational network for communications, coalescing related educational efforts, developing leadership, and effecting change. The Coalition should monitor and report on state efforts to promote information literacy and resource-based learning and provide recognition of individuals and programs for their exemplary information literacy efforts.

   The Coalition should be organized with an advisory committee made up of nationally prominent public figures from librarianship, education, business, and government. The responsibilities of the advisory committee should include support for Coalition efforts in the areas of capturing media attention, raising public awareness, and fostering a climate favorable for information literacy. In addition, the advisory committee should actively seek funding to promote research and demonstration projects.

3. Research and demonstration projects related to information and its use need to be undertaken. To date, remarkably little research has been done to understand how information can be more effectively managed to meet educational and societal objectives or to explore how information management skills impact on overall school and academic perfor-

mance. What research does exist appears primarily in library literature, which is seldom read by educators or state decision makers.

For future efforts to be successful, a national research agenda should be developed and implemented. The number of issues needing to be addressed are significant and should include the following:

- What are the social effects of reading?
- With electronic media eclipsing reading for many people, what will be the new place of the printed word?
- How do the characteristics of information resources (format, length, age) affect their usefulness?
- How does the use of information vary by discipline?
- How does access to information impact on the effectiveness of citizen action groups?
- How do information management skills affect student performance and retention?
- What role can information management skills play in the economic and social advancement of minorities?

Also needed is research that will promote a "sophisticated understanding of the full range of the issues and processes related to the generation, distribution, and use of information so that libraries can fulfill their obligations to their users and potential users and so that research and scholarship in all fields can flourish."[12]

The Coalition can play a major role in obtaining funding for such research and for fostering demonstration projects that can provide fertile ground for controlled experiments that can contrast benefits from traditional versus resource-based learning opportunities for students.

4. State Departments of Education, Commissions on Higher Education, and Academic Governing Boards should be responsible to ensure that a climate conducive to students' becoming information literate exists in their states and on their campuses.

Of importance are two complementary issues: the development of an information literate citizenry and the move from textbook and lecture style learning to resource-based learning. The latter is, in fact, the means to the former as well as to producing lifelong, independent, and self-directed learners. As is appropriate within their stated missions, such bodies are urged to do the following:

- To incorporate the spirit and intent of information literacy into curricular requirements, recommendations, and instructional materials. (Two excellent models for state school guidelines are Washington's "Information Skills Curriculum Guide: Process Scope and Sequence" and "Library Information Skills: Guide for Oregon Schools K-12.")

- To incorporate into professional preparation and in-service training for teachers an appreciation for the importance of resource-based learning, to encourage implementation of it in their subject areas, and to provide opportunities to master implementation techniques.
- To encourage and support coordination of school/campus and public library resources/services with classroom instruction in offering resource-based learning.
- To include coverage of information literacy competencies in state assessment examinations.
- To establish recognition programs of exemplary projects for learning information management skills in elementary and secondary schools, in higher education institutions, and in professional preparation programs.

5. Teacher education and performance expectations should be modified to include information literacy concerns. Inherent in the concepts of information literacy and resource-based learning is the complementary concept of the teacher as a facilitator of student learning rather than as presenter of ready-made information. To be successful in such roles, teachers should make use of an expansive array of information resources. They should be familiar with and able to use selected databases, learning networks, reference materials, textbooks, journals, newspapers, magazines, and other resources. They also should place a premium on problem solving and see that their classrooms are extended outward to encompass the learning resources of the library media centers and the community. They also should expect their students to become information literate.

To encourage the development of teachers who are facilitators of learning, the following recommendations are made to schools of teacher education. Those responsible for in-service teacher training should also evaluate current capabilities of teaching professionals and incorporate the following recommendations into their programs as needed:

- New knowledge from cognitive research on thinking skills should be incorporated into pedagogical skills development.
- Integral to all programs should be instruction in managing the classroom, individualizing instruction, setting problems, questioning, promoting cooperative learning—all of which should rely on case studies and information resources of the entire school and community.
- Instruction within the disciplines needs to emphasize a problem-solving approach and the development of a sophisticated level of information management skills appropriate to the individual disciplines.

- School library media specialists need to view the instructional goals of their schools as an integral part of their own concern and responsibilities and should actively contribute toward the ongoing professional development of teachers and principals. They should be members of curriculum and instructional teams and provide leadership in integrating appropriate information and educational technologies into school programming. (For further recommendations regarding the role of library media specialists, consult *Information Power: Guidelines for School Media Programs* prepared by the American Association of School Librarians and the Association for Educational Communications and Technology, 1988.)
- Exit requirements from teacher education programs should include each candidate's ability to use selected databases, networks, reference materials, administrative and instructional software packages, and new forms of learning technologies.
- A portion of the practicum or teaching experience of beginning teachers should be spent with library media specialists. These opportunities should be based in the school library media center to promote an understanding of resources available in both that facility and other community libraries and to emphasize the concepts and skills necessary to become a learning facilitator.
- Cooperative, or supervising, teachers who can demonstrate their commitment to thinking skills instruction and information literacy should be matched with student teachers, and teachers who see themselves as learning facilitators should be relied upon to serve as role models. Student teachers should also have the opportunity to observe and practice with a variety of models for the teaching of critical thinking.

6. An understanding of the relationship of information literacy to the themes of the White House Conference on Library and Information Services should be promoted. The White House conference themes of literacy, productivity, and democracy will provide a unique opportunity to foster public awareness of the importance of information literacy. . . . The American Library Association and the Coalition on Information Literacy should aggressively promote consideration of information literacy within state deliberations as well as within the White House conference itself.

BACKGROUND TO REPORT

The American Library Association's Presidential Committee on Information Literacy was appointed in 1987 by ALA President Margaret Chisholm with three expressed purposes: (1) to define information literacy within the higher literacies and its importance to student performance, lifelong learning, and active citizenship; (2) to design one or more models for information literacy development appropriate to formal and informal learning environments throughout people's lifetimes; and (3) to determine implications for the continuing education and development of teachers. The Committee, which consists of leaders in education and librarianship, has worked actively to accomplish its mission since its establishment. Members of the Committee include the following:

Gordon M. Ambach, Executive Director
Council of Chief State School Officers

William L. Bainbridge, President
School Match

Patricia Senn Breivik, Chair, Director
Auraria Library, University of Colorado at Denver

Rexford Brown, Director
Policies and the Higher Literacies Project
Education Commission of the States

Judith S. Eaton, President
Community College of Philadelphia

David Imig, Executive Director
American Association of Colleges for Teacher Education

Sally Kilgore, Professor
Emory University
(former Director of the Office of Research, U.S. Department of Education)

Carol Kuhlthau, Director
Educational Media Services Programs
Rutgers University

Joseph Mika, Director
Library Science Program
Wayne State University

Richard D. Miller, Executive Director
American Association of School Administrators

Roy D. Miller, Executive Assistant to the Director
Brooklyn Public Library

Sharon J. Rogers, University Librarian
George Washington University

Robert Wedgeworth, Dean
School of Library Service
Columbia University

This report was released on January 10, 1989, in Washington, D.C.

FURTHER INFORMATION

Further information on information literacy can be obtained from

Information Literacy and K-12
c/o American Association of School Librarians
American Library Association
50 East Huron Street
Chicago, IL 60611

Information Literacy and Higher Education
c/o Association of College and Research Libraries
American Library Association
50 East Huron Street
Chicago, IL 60611

REFERENCES

1. Terrell H. Bell, Communication to CU President E. Gordon Gee, September 1986.
2. Herbert E. Meyer, *Real World Intelligence: Organized Information for Executives* (New York: Weidenfeld & Nicholson, 1987), p. 24.
3. James B. Tchobanoff, "The Impact Approach: Value as Measured by the Benefit of the Information Professional to the Parent Organization," in *President's Task Force on the Value of the Information Professional* (Anaheim, Calif: Special Libraries Assn., June 10, 1987), p. 47.
4. Harlan Cleveland, *The Knowledge Executive: Leadership in an Information Society* (New York: Dutton, 1985), p. xviii.
5. Joan C. Durrance, *Armed for Action: Library Response to Citizen Information Needs* (New York: Neal-Schuman, 1984), p. ix.
6. Major Owens, "State Government and Libraries," *Library Journal* 101 (January 1976): 27.
7. United States National Commission on Excellence in Education, *A Nation at Risk: The Imperative for Educational Reform* (Washington, DC: U.S. Government Printing Office, 1983).
8. Frank Newman, *Higher Education and the American Resurgence* (Princeton, NJ: Princeton University Press, 1985), p. 152.
9. Ernest L. Boyer, *College: The Undergraduate Experience in America* (New York: Harper & Row, 1987).
10. "Prologue and Major Recommendations of Carnegie Foundation's Report on Colleges," *Chronicle of Higher Education* 33 (5 November 1986): 10-11.

11. K. Patricia Cross, "A Proposal to Improve Teaching or What Taking Teaching Seriously Should Mean," *AAHE Bulletin* 39 (September 1986): 10-11.
12. Edward Connery Lathem, ed., *American Libraries as Centers of Scholarship* (Hanover, NH: Dartmouth College, 1978), p.58.

INFORMATION LITERACY BIBLIOGRAPHY

Patricia Senn Breivik, "Making the Most of Libraries in the Search for Academic Excellence," *Change* (July/August 1987) 19: 44-52.

Patricia Senn Breivik and Robert Wedgeworth, *Libraries and the Search for Academic Excellence*. Metuchen, NJ.: Scarecrow Press, 1988. Papers from a National Symposium sponsored by Columbia University and the University of Colorado, New York, March 15-17, 1987.

Larry Hardesty, Nicholas P. Lovfich, Jr., and James Mannon, "Library Use Instruction: Assessment of the Long-Term Effects," *College & Research Libraries* (January 1982) 43: 38-46.

James A. Hyatt and Aurora A. Santiago, *University Libraries in Transition*. Washington, D.C.: National Association of College and University Business Officers, 1987.

David W. Lewis, "Inventing the Electronic University," *College & Research Libraries* (July 1988) 49: 291-304.

"The Literacy Gap," *Time*, December 19, 1988: 56-57.

Barbara B. Moran, *Academic Libraries: The Changing Knowledge Center of Colleges and Universities*. ASHE-ERIC Higher Education Research Report, No. 8. Washington, DC: Association for the Study of Higher Education, 1984.

APPENDIX B

National Forum on Information Literacy Membership List

This list is current as of May 1997.

ABC News Interactive

American Association for Adult Continuing Education

American Association for Higher Education

American Association of Colleges for Teacher Education

American Association of Community Colleges

American Association of School Administrators

American Association of School Librarians

American Association of University Professors

American Library Association

American Society for Public Administration

Association for Educational Communications and Technology

Association for Library and Information Science Education

Association for Supervision and Curriculum Development

Association of American Colleges and Universities

Association of American Publishers

Association of College & Research Libraries

Association of Public Data Users

Association of Specialized and Cooperative Library Agencies

Center for Law and Education, Inc.

Chief Officers of State Library Agencies

College Board

Commission on Higher Education of the Middle States Association of Colleges and Schools

Consortium for School Networking

Council of Chief State School Officers

Council of Independent Colleges

Education Commission of the States

EDUCOM

ERIC Clearinghouse on Information Resources

Friends of Libraries U.S.A.

Hispanic Policy Development Project

Information Industry Association

International Visual Literacy Association

Literacy Volunteers of America

National Alliance of Black School Educators

National Association of Counties

National Association of Partners in Education

National Association of Secondary School Principals

National Association of State Boards of Education

National Association of State Directors of Vocational Education

National Association of State Educational Media Professionals

National Commission on Libraries & Information Science

National Community Education Association

National Conference of State Legislatures

National Consumers League

National Council for the Social Studies

National Council of Teachers of English

National Council of Teachers of Mathematics

National Education Association

National Forum for Black Public Administrators

National Governors' Association

National School Boards Association

National Science Teachers Association

Newspaper Association of America Foundation

Office of Educational Research and Improvement (U.S. Department of Education)

People for the American Way

Public Library Association

Special Libraries Association

State Higher Education Executive Officers

U.S. Small Business Administration

Women in Communications, Inc.

APPENDIX C

Data Collection on Information Literacy Programs at Higher Education Institutions

Analysis and Report by the Association of College and Research Libraries, 1994-1995

Since the release of the American Library Association Presidential Committee Final Report on Information Literacy in 1989, a great deal has been written about the benefits of information literacy; however, little of this literature has actually surveyed and measured the extent to which information literacy has been assimilated into the curriculum of our post-secondary institutions. In 1994-1995, as an outgrowth of the National Forum on Information Literacy, the Association of College and Research Libraries (ACRL), in collaboration with the Commission on Higher Education (CHE) of the Middle States Association of Colleges and Schools and the Western Accrediting Commission for Senior Colleges and Universities (WASC), explored this question by conducting a national survey of the 3,236 accredited U.S. colleges and universities within the six regional accrediting agencies. 834 institutions responded to the survey, which was endorsed by the American Association of Higher Education.

From the five specific questions asked, it was hoped that a snapshot-in-time profile of the status of different aspects of information literacy on campuses might emerge. The address files of the six regional accrediting agencies were used as mailing lists for the surveys, and the mailings were addressed to the accrediting agencies' campus contact (usually presidents, deans or provosts) with instructions for the survey to be routed to those best suited to respond. Entitled *Data Collection on Information Literacy Programs at USA Higher Education Institutions*, the survey stated that it was seeking data on information literacy efforts that bring about the integration of information resources and technology into the curriculum, not on traditional library instruction efforts. The survey provided the following definition: "Information literacy is defined as a subset of critical thinking skills which consist of individuals' abilities to know when they have an informational need and to access, evaluate, and effectively use information." The survey also indicated that the results would be published and would be used to identify programs that could be highlighted at regional and national conferences and in professional publications.

The survey asked the following five numbered questions with a space to check YES or NO:

1. Does your campus have a functional information literacy program? (If so, please attach documentation on the program or briefly describe its goals and objectives and how it fits into the curriculum.)
2. Does your campus offer a course that focuses on the development of information literacy abilities? (Please attach syllabus.)
3. Are information literacy learning experiences integrated into courses in all majors? (Please attach some sample syllabi.)
4. Are there formal assessments of students' information literacy performance? (Please attach documentation or briefly describe.)
5. Are there faculty and staff development efforts provided to undergird the information literacy program on your campus? (Please attach documentation and briefly describe.)

Surveys sent to the Middle States Association of Colleges and Schools and the Western Accrediting Commission for Senior Colleges and Universities were requested to be returned by December 31, 1994. All other surveys were to be returned to ACRL by either March 28 or June 1, 1995.

LIMITATIONS OF DATA

Examination of the 834 responses revealed that some institutions' definitions of information literacy may have differed from the definition stated in the survey. Despite statements to the contrary, some of the respondents associated information literacy with computer literacy or more classic forms of library or bibliographic instruction. Thus, differing understandings of information literacy may have affected some of the responses.

The wording of the first question may also have confused some of the respondents. Specifically, the phrase "a functional information literacy program" may have been too broad because the words "functional" and "program" could have varying degrees of interpretation.

Some of the questions did not allow institutions that were on the verge of revamping or introducing information literacy programs to respond. This circumstance may have prevented a number of institutions from answering YES to more of the questions.

Finally, the question that asked if information literacy was incorporated into all majors at the institution may have screened out numerous respondents who had excellent programs in some or most of their majors.

RESULTS

Of the institutions surveyed, 26 percent responded to the survey. Of the 834 respondents, 261 were from the Middle States Association, 214 from the North Central, 192 from the Southern, 85 from the Western, 46 from the North Western, and 36 from New England (Fig. 1).

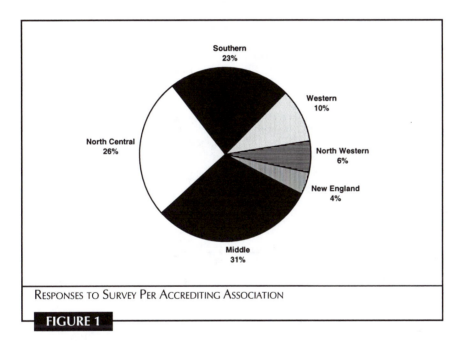

RESPONSES TO SURVEY PER ACCREDITING ASSOCIATION

FIGURE 1

The breakdown by type of institution indicated that most of the respondents were 2-Year or Comprehensive, followed by 4-Year, University, Graduate, and Upper-Level (Fig. 2). Figure 2 closely resembles a pie chart (Fig.2.1) published in *Peterson's Register of Higher Education* (1996, 12) which breaks down higher education institutions by their type to indicate that the responding institutions are a representative sampling of U.S. campuses.

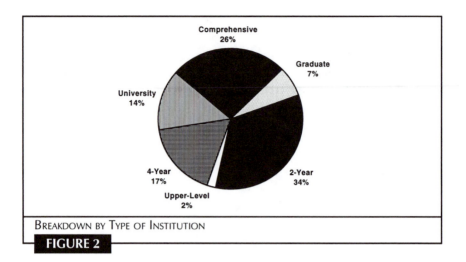

BREAKDOWN BY TYPE OF INSTITUTION

FIGURE 2

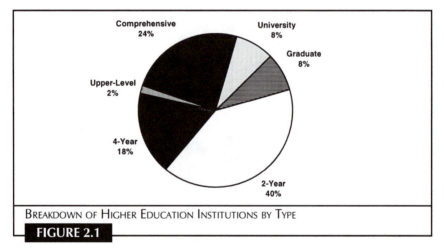

BREAKDOWN OF HIGHER EDUCATION INSTITUTIONS BY TYPE

FIGURE 2.1

Affirmative responses to the five questions are shown by Figure 3. Almost 22 percent of the total respondents had a functional information literacy program. Exactly 25 percent offered a course that focuses on information literacy abilities. Affirmative responses to Question 3, which asked if information literacy learning experiences were integrated into courses in all majors, were 17 percent of the total number of responses. Similarly, 17 percent answered affirmatively to Question 4, which asked if there are formal assessments of students' information literacy performances. Question 5, which asked if faculty and staff development efforts are provided to undergird the information literacy program on campus, had the most affirmative answers with a percentage of 29 percent.

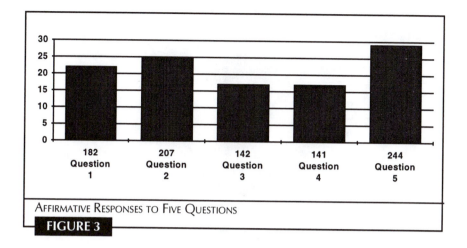

AFFIRMATIVE RESPONSES TO FIVE QUESTIONS

FIGURE 3

Thirty-three institutions answered YES to all five questions, but only 27 sent attachments with their surveys. Figure 4 illustrates how these 33 respondents broke down by type of institution.

Thus, 4 percent of the institutions indicated that they had functional programs; a course that focuses on information literacy, courses integrated into all majors; assessment of student performance, and faculty and staff involvement in development efforts. However, in contrast to this, 459 institutions, 55 percent, answered NO to all five questions. Figure 5 illustrates the breakdown by type of institution.

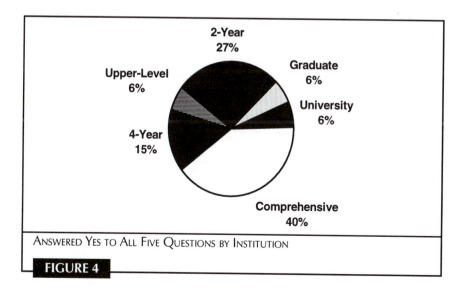

ANSWERED YES TO ALL FIVE QUESTIONS BY INSTITUTION

FIGURE 4

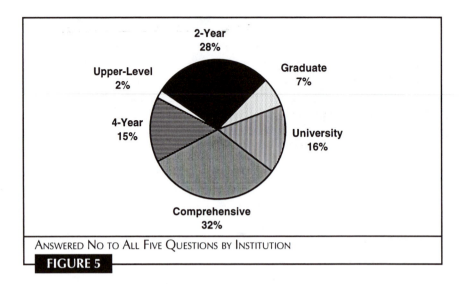

2-Year
28%

Upper-Level
2%

Graduate
7%

4-Year
15%

University
16%

Comprehensive
32%

ANSWERED NO TO ALL FIVE QUESTIONS BY INSTITUTION
FIGURE 5

Table 1 presents how institutional types responded affirmatively to each of the five questions asked in the survey.

TABLE 1

AFFIRMATIVE ANSWERS TO FIVE QUESTIONS BY INSTITUTIONAL TYPE

Institutional Type	Functional Programs	Offers an IL Course	Integrated in Majors	Assess IL Skills	Faculty Development
2-Year	51	56	47	45	79
Upper-Level	3	2	4	3	2
4-Year	28	23	25	20	32
Comprehensive	59	66	42	38	80
University	29	44	15	24	37
Graduation	12	16	9	11	14
Total	182	207	142	141	244

Figure 6 illustrates numerous combinations of certain questions. There were 182 positive responses to Question 1 but only 99 to Questions 1 and 2, indicating that over 80 respondents had a literacy program but no course focusing on the development of information literacy abilities. Only 88 institutions were able to answer YES to having both a functional program and the integration of information literacy into all majors. Only 91 institutions had

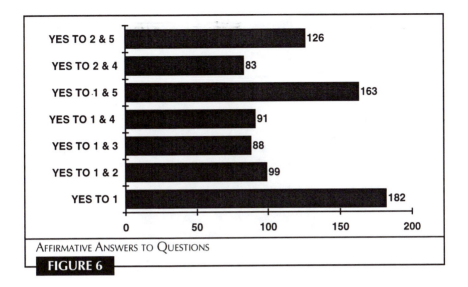

AFFIRMATIVE ANSWERS TO QUESTIONS

FIGURE 6

both a functional program and formal assessments of students. However, 163 institutions had a functional program and faculty and staff development efforts to undergird their program on campus. Eighty-three institutions have a course that focuses on information literacy and gives formal assessments of students' work. Those with a course and faculty and staff development efforts numbered 126.

When the respondents to the five questions from Table 1 are displayed graphically (Fig. 7) by institutional type, they provide some interesting comparisons. There were 182 affirmative responses to Question 1 out of 834 responses (22 percent).

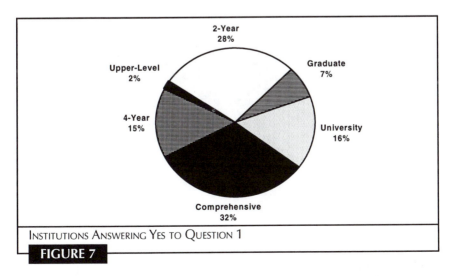

INSTITUTIONS ANSWERING YES TO QUESTION 1

FIGURE 7

Question 2 had 207 affirmative responses, 25 percent of the total responses. More universities had a specific course that focused on development of information literacy skills (Fig. 8) than had a functional information literacy program (Fig. 7). Comprehensive and 2-Year percentages remained about the same.

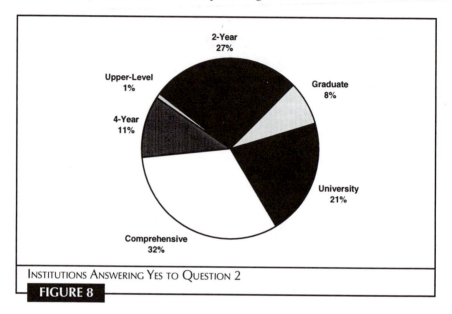

INSTITUTIONS ANSWERING YES TO QUESTION 2

FIGURE 8

Two-year institutions had the best percentage of the 142 affirmative responses to Question 3, which asked if the institution had information literacy integrated into all majors (Fig. 9).

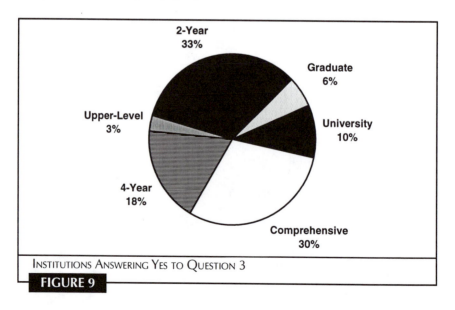

INSTITUTIONS ANSWERING YES TO QUESTION 3

FIGURE 9

The distribution of institutions in Question 4, which asked about formal assessments of students' performance (Fig. 10), demonstrates that universities and graduate schools have more participation in testing than in incorporating information literacy into all majors.

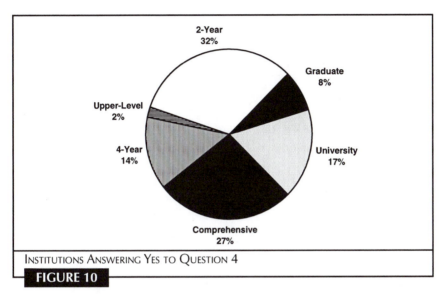

INSTITUTIONS ANSWERING YES TO QUESTION 4

FIGURE 10

The affirmative answers to Question 5 (faculty and staff development efforts) by institution type indicate that Comprehensive and 2-Year institutions make up the largest part of the pie (Fig. 11). Overall, this question had the best positive response with 29 percent of the 834 respondents indicating that they have faculty and staff involved in information literacy development efforts.

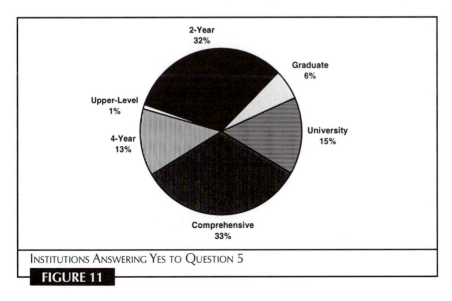

INSTITUTIONS ANSWERING YES TO QUESTION 5

FIGURE 11

ANALYSIS OF DATA AND EXAMPLES OF PROGRAMS

Progress has been made towards integrating information literacy into post-secondary institutions. Over 22 percent of responding institutions reported a functional information literacy program and 25 percent offered a course that focused on the development of those abilities. Even more encouraging was the fact that 29 percent of those surveyed had faculty and staff development efforts provided to undergird the information literacy program on campus.

However, the survey indicated that during the winter of 1994/spring of 1995, many institutions had not yet implemented information literacy into their curriculums. 459 institutions, or 55 percent of those surveyed, responded negatively to all five questions. Even if Question 3, which concerned information literacy integration into all majors, was removed from the set of five questions, only 52 respondents or 6 percent could answer yes to Questions 1, 2, 4, and 5. Thus, the nationwide picture of program implementation provided by the survey shows that information literacy is still in its infancy.

Question 5, which queried the presence of faculty and staff development efforts, had more YES answers (Fig. 3) than the other four questions. This result may be interpreted to indicate that a number of institutions were in the process of developing their programs or were about to introduce them in the near future. Also, institutions with functional programs and faculty and staff development efforts (Questions 1 & 5) had more affirmative responses than institutions with a specific course and faculty and staff development efforts (Questions 2 & 5) (Fig. 6). Thus, those with functional programs had a greater propensity for faculty and staff involvement.

More institutions have a course that focuses on information literacy than have a functional program (Fig. 3). However, those that have functional programs are more likely to answer YES to Questions 4 and 5, which address testing and staff and faculty development (Fig. 6).

Figure 2 breaks down the respondents to this survey by type of institution. The pie chart shows that 34 percent of the 834 respondents are 2-year, 26 percent Comprehensive, 17 percent 4-Year, 14 percent University, 7 percent Graduate, and 2 percent Upper-Level. The first major deviation from these numbers is seen in Figure 4, which illustrates the breakdown of the 33 institutions that affirmatively answered all five questions. This chart indicates that more comprehensive institutions (40 percent) fit the information literacy model indicated in the survey. The comprehensive institutions made up the majority of the affirmative responses in all five questions except Questions 3 (Fig. 9) and 4 (Fig. 10). The 2-Year institutions had the most favorable responses to Question 3, which asked if information literacy was integrated into all majors, and Question 4, which asked if students were tested. The 2-Year institutions were only one percentage point behind Comprehensives in Question 5 (Fig. 11) regarding faculty development efforts.

The results of this survey show a promising start and illustrate that institutions of all types have been successful in incorporating information literacy programs into their curricula. A few examples of these programs are summarized in this appendix.

One 2-Year institution in the Southern accrediting region identified information literacy as one of its seven general education outcomes. This institution specified that graduates would be able to independently gather and stay abreast of current developments in their field of specialization. Students will be able to identify appropriate information needs, access and retrieve the information, evaluate its relevance, and use it in personal and professional decision making. One course specifically focused on information literacy skills also serves as an orientation to the college experience. The college then continues to develop skills through courses that have assignment-related instruction focusing on subject-specific resources. Subject-specific resource guides are given to the students and include both print and electronic (Internet) formats. The performance of the student is assessed by surveys of alumni and enrolled students as well as by reviewing worksheets. The Educational Resources staff works with the faculty to raise their awareness of the importance of teaching information literacy. Workshops are also given.

A comprehensive institution in the North Central region has two informational literacy programs. One program uses print and electronic resources to take maximum advantage of resources to meet informational needs. Objectives include defining a suitable research topic, identifying and effectively using appropriate access tools, and evaluating the specific resources. The other program focuses on technology literacy and is taught by a division of the Media Center. This program provides learning opportunities for students in areas of computing and information technology, provides classroom support for faculty to integrate computing and information technology into their curricula, and collaborates with Information Technology Units to provide support to students using computing and information technology. This institution also has two departments that offer courses that focus on information literacy abilities. The Library Media Department in the School of Education offers courses that include an Internet component. The Computer Science Department also offers a course. Most majors have courses with information literacy learning components. Formal assessment is accomplished in three of the courses. Faculty and staff development is accomplished through workshops and conferences.

Another comprehensive institution from the North Central region adopted information literacy and decided that it should be a shared responsibility of the teaching faculty and the Information Technologies and Resources staff. The faculty would be responsible for teaching critical thinking skills and effective use of information, while Information Technologies staff served as facilitators in providing information access and management. No specific course focuses on the development of information literacy skills, but each discipline is charged with developing the courses and content that meet the general education requirement. There is no specific evaluation procedure. Faculty and staff are encouraged to participate in information literacy programs given by Information Technologies.

Finally, a four-year institution in the New England accrediting region has adopted a program that highlights the teaching role of the library in the liberal arts curriculum. This program promotes the teaching of critical thinking skills for evaluating information as well as the teaching of skills for effective and efficient information access, especially of computer-based resources. This has been accomplished by a partnership between the library and faculty. All academic departments have at least one course-integrated library component in addition to all the library components that are in 22 to 24 required first-year seminars.

CONCLUSION

This 1994/1995 survey set out to measure the extent to which institutions have adopted information literacy programs as a means of preparing their students for this information rich environment. The results from the survey clearly show that information literacy is being pursued in varying degrees by 22% to 25% of the respondents. This might be considered clear progress; the ALA Presidential Committee on Information Literacy only made its recommendations in 1989. However, there were some unsettling aspects to this survey.

459 institutions (55%) answered NO to all five questions, indicating that these institutions had not yet assimilated information literacy into their curriculum. Secondly, a number of the institutions that answered YES to Questions 1 or 2 had confused information literacy with computer literacy or bibliographic instruction. Information literacy is more than the incorporation of technology and computers into the classroom. It is also more than simply training students how to use bibliographic tools that access information in the library. Rather, information literacy is a resource-based learning process that fosters students' abilities to identify, locate, evaluate, and use information from a myriad of sources both technological and print. It also fosters active learning by teaching students to critically analyze and synthesize this information.[1] With continuing efforts by the regional accrediting agencies and the growing number of campus-initiated undertakings, it is reasonable to assume that the number of campuses with no information literacy initiatives would be smaller if resurveyed and that the meaning of information literacy would be more broadly understood.

NOTE

1. D.W. Farmer, "Information Literacy: Developing Students as Independent Learners," *New Directions for Higher Education*, No. 78 (San Francisco: Jossey-Bass Publishers, Summer, 1992), p. 2.

APPENDIX D

Writing Syllabus for Wheaton College Psychology 212a

Psychology 212a—1996   Mr. Zuriff
Perception   330 Knapton

WRITING SYLLABUS

This course is writing intensive. This means that in addition to learning about perception, the content area of the course, you will also learn something about writing. In particular, this course is designed to teach you how to write what is known as a "literature review paper." To write such a paper, one reads various sources about a particular topic and then integrates what one has read into a paper that summarizes, discusses, and analyzes the topic. Writing a literature review is useful not only in psychology and in college, but you will find the skills you learn helpful in later life whenever you have to research a topic thoroughly.

In acquiring these skills you will learn how to

1. explore a topic in depth
2. use library research resources
3. read primary sources in psychology
4. organize your thoughts in writing

Many subskills contribute to proficiency in writing a literature review paper, and the course is designed to teach you each subskill separately. You will be given an assignment for each skill, feedback on your work, and the opportunity to revise your work based on that feedback. By the end of the course, you will have mastered the necessary subskills and be ready to write your final product. Because each step builds on the previous one, it is important that you stay on schedule.

September 10   Hand in a one-page reaction paper. You will have read one article on your topic, and this paper should present your preliminary thoughts. First, define the topic and the perceptual phenomenon you are studying. Perhaps you can give everyday examples. Then informally discuss your reactions to your topic. For example, what do you hope to learn about it? Do you have any ideas of your own about how to explain the phenomenon? Did you find the article interesting? Why or Why not? How hard was the article to understand? What about it made it difficult for you? This paper will not be graded; you may collaborate with others in your group.

September 12   Class will meet in the library where you will learn about *PsychLit*, a computer-assisted search method that will enable you to find articles on your topic in psychology journals.

September 17   Hand in a 2-page summary, in your own words (understandable to someone who has taken Psych 101), of an article on your topic. Preferably, this should be an article that you have located through *PsychLit*, but if you cannot do that, then use the article you were originally given. Be sure the article reports a study and is not a review article. This summary should describe: (1) the purpose of the study, (2) the method used [a. the subject's task, b. the apparatus, c. the variable manipulated], and (3) the results. Collaboration is encouraged.

October 1   Hand in: (1) a revision of your summary based on the feedback you have received; (2) the first draft you already handed in; (3) a bibliography, in APA style (see the Jolley book), of at least 10 articles you have found on your topic. Besides your *PsychLit* search, another way to find articles is to look at the reference list at the end of the articles you have already found. This will include additional references that may be relevant. Use *PsychLit* to get a print-out of the abstracts for these references; (4) the *PsychLit* print-out, indicating clearly the ones that you have selected for inclusion in your bibliography. Make sure the articles are in English, accessible, and understandable to you. No collaboration.

October 8   Hand in: (1) one-page summary of a second article on your topic. You will have to be concise; (2) a one-paragraph summary of this article. You have to be even more concise; (3) a revision of your bibliography based on feedback received. No collaboration.

October 29 Hand in a 3-page paper reviewing the theoretical issues in your topic. What are the explanations psychologists have offered for the perceptual phenomenon? How do the explanations differ? Which experiments support which theory? If there are no theoretical issues, write your paper on the variables that have been shown to affect the phenomenon. Which experiments show these effects? What controversies are there about these effects? For either type of paper, you do not need to describe the experiments in detail. A sentence or paragraph is sufficient. Also be sure to use the APA citation format. No collaboration.

November 19 Now you are ready to integrate what you have learned about library research, reading journals, summarizing articles, and evaluating theoretical issues and independent variables. Hand in a first draft of your literature review. This should be: (1) 8 to 12 pages long; (2) cite 5 to 10 references; (3) include an APA style bibliography at the end. No collaboration. Here are some guidelines:

A. Be sure to cite references properly (see the Jolley book). If you present something you have read as if it is your own, that is plagiarism. If you merely paraphrase what you have read without really understanding it, you are not doing the assignment properly.

B. For a grade between C– and C+, you can merely summarize each of the articles in succession.

C. For a grade between B– and B+, you need to integrate successfully what you have read and organize it along thematic lines. For example, one way to organize your paper is:

1. definition of the topic and the perceptual phenomenon
2. examples of the phenomenon (everyday and experimental)
3. methods used to study it, citing examples
4. variables that affect it, citing examples
5. theories proposed to explain it

D. For a grade between A– and A+ you need not only to successfully integrate the material but also to add some of your own original thought. For example, you might evaluate the various studies, or say which theories you think are best supported by the studies, or even suggest an original way of looking at the topic.

E. Your paper will be evaluated for grammar, writing style, organization, and spelling.

December 10 Hand in revised final draft of literature review paper along with your first draft.

APPENDIX E

King's College Competency Growth Plan in Library and Information Literacy for Students Majoring in Marketing

Competency Description	FRESHMAN Strategy	Asessment Criteria
The student will be able to locate, understand, and use the major facilities, services, and research tools of the library: card catalog, periodical indexes, reference works, microfilm readers, interlibrary loans and reference librarians. The student will be able to use the MLA Style of Documentation.	*Basic Library Skills Workbook* completed in CORE 100 and CORE 110 during the fall semester. **CORE 110: Effective Writing** The student will write at least one paper requiring research.	1. The Student completes with a grade of "Pass" the worksheets supplied with the *Basic Library Skills Workbook*. • to identify the physical layout of the library; • to identify the Dewey Decimal System of Classification used by the library; • to locate encyclopedias and dictionaries; • to use the catalog and union catalogs; • to identify and use Library of Congress subject headings;

FRESHMAN		
Competency Description	**Strategy**	**Assessment Criteria**
		• to locate and use periodicals and periodical indexes, newspapers and newspaper indexes, book review indexes, and dictionaries.
		2. The student develops and implements a simple search strategy.
		3. The student distinguishes sources that provide facts that present opinions, e.g., explains the difference between general and specialized dictionaries and encyclopedias.
		4. The student compares and contrasts sources and discovers points of agreement
		5. The student recognizes an author's ownership of an idea or opinion.
		6. The student distinguishes popular from scholarly material.
		7. The student records bibliographic information and creates a correct bibliographic citation.
		8. The student correctly uses and cites sources in at least one of the papers required in CORE 110.

SOPHOMORE		
Competency Description	**Strategy**	**Assessment Criteria**
The student will be able to identify, locate, select, analyze, and use appropriate company, industry, product, market, and demographic information.	***MKT 210: Principles of Marketing*** Preparation of a Marketing Plan or simulation for a particular industry and/or product.	1. The student identifies the types of information needed to identify and locate appropriate materials. 2. The student develops a research strategy, identifying potential problems with alternative strategies. 3. The student evaluates the information located in terms of its appropriateness, currency, depth, and authority of its source. 4. The student validates information, when necessary, through other sources. 5. The student synthesizes the collected information, draws valid conclusions, and documents the evidence presented to support each position taken in the Marketing Plan.

JUNIOR/SENIOR		
Competency Description	**Strategy**	**Assessment Criteria**
The student will be able to use library resources appropriate to advertising. The student will be able to use library resources appropriate to international marketing.	***MKT 360: Creative Advertising*** Preparation of an Advertising Plan which includes current statistical and other reference information ***MKT 390: International Marketing*** Preparation of a marketing feasibility study for introducing a product in a selected foreign country.	1. The student uses CD-ROM and computerized literature sources to locate information. 2. The student uses reference services by recognizing librarians as resource guides and interpreters. 3. The student uses library and information technology to access cultural, social, political, and economic data for a selected foreign country for the purpose of making a marketing decision.

SENIOR		
Competency Description	**Strategy**	**Assessment Criteria**
The student will be able to design and implement sophisticated search strategies to conduct marketing research to support a Marketing Plan.	***MKT 480: Marketing Management*** Preparation of a Marketing Plan at a professional level for the introduction of a new product.	1. The student designs a comprehensive search strategy. 2. The student synthesizes data from a variety of sources and presents it in appropriate and relevant formats (charts, graphs, matrices, etc.) to support a Marketing Plan.

SELECTED
RESOURCES

LOEX

Easy access to existing models is available through many state and regional clearinghouses and through Library Orientation Exchange (LOEX), a national depository of library instruction materials located in Ypsilanti, Michigan. LOEX also sponsors annual conferences on library instruction at various locations in the United States.

LOEX Clearinghouse for Library Instruction
University Library
Eastern Michigan University
Ypsilanti, MI 48197
Telephone: (313) 487-0168
Fax: (313) 487-8861
E-mail: <LibShirato@emuvax.emich.edu>

ERIC CLEARINGHOUSE ON INFORMATION & TECHNOLOGY

ERIC/IT is one of 16 clearinghouses in the Educational Resources Information Clearinghouse (ERIC) system with expertise in library and information science and educational technology. Researchers who use Information Literacy as an ERIC search term will find many citations listed for the literature in this field. Users needing additional online searching assistance can e-mail AskERIC <askeric@ericir.syr.edu> and receive a detailed response within two business days. The ERIC/IT website <http://ericir.syr.edu/ithome> includes links to professional organizations specializing in information literacy issues. ERIC/ IT also publishes monographs and digests about information literacy in all levels of education.

ERIC Clearinghouse on Information & Technology
Syracuse University
4-194 Center for Science & Technology
Syracuse, NY 13244-4100
Telephone: (315) 443-3640 or 1-800-464-9107
Fax: (315) 443-5488
ERIC/IT e-mail: eric@ericir.syr.edu
URL: http://ericir.syr.edu/ithome
AskERIC e-mail: askeric@ericir.syr.edu
AskERIC URL: http://ericir.syr.edu

ASSOCIATION OF COLLEGE AND RESEARCH LIBRARIES (ACRL)

ACRL is an 11,000-member division of the American Library Association. Inquiries to its headquarters can provide information on existing materials and information literacy experts.

Association of College and Research Libraries
50 E. Huron Street
Chicago, IL 60611-2795
Telephone: (800) 545-2433
Fax: (312) 280-2520
E-mail: <ACRL-FRM@oicvm.vic.edu>

ERIC CLEARINGHOUSE ON INFORMATION RESOURCES TOP ELEVEN INFORMATION LITERACY SITES ON THE WORLD WIDE WEB

Big Six Skills Homepage
<http://edweb.sdsu.edu/edfirst/bigsix/bigsix.html>
Based on the work of Mike Eisenberg and Bob Berkowitz, this site provides explanations and links about information problem-solving and information literacy. Includes an overview of the Big Six Skills, instructional units (including the design of instruction), a glossary of terms, and additional resources.

Calico INFOLIT Homepage
<http://www.sun.ac.za/local/library/calico/infolit/>
This site in South Africa provides information on a variety of research and pilot projects undertaken by the Cape Library Cooperative to encourage the

development of information literacy in the five schools of higher learning in the Western Cape. This detailed site includes links to other sites.

California State University at Cal Poly
< http://www.lib.calpoly.edu./infocomp/index.html>

This site provides a focal point for the Information Competence initiatives within the California State University system. The site includes 10 modules for teaching information competency.

Info Zone
< http://www.mbnet.mb.ca/~mstimson/>

Designed primarily for high school students, this site identifies each of the steps involved in a research project. Under each step students find a list of Internet links to sites that will help them master that skill. For instance, under "understanding and appraising information," students find links to Web-based sources that give them advice on evaluating various types of information. Info Zone also includes links to other information skill sites.

Information Literacy Home Page
< http:www.fiu.eduf~library/iti/index/html>

Created and maintained by Florida International University Libraries, this site provides information about local and national efforts to implement information literacy efforts into a variety of curricula.

Information Literacy Group
< http://www.ucalgary.ca/library/ILG/index.html>

This University of Calgary site offers an excellent list of links to Internet resources, as well as descriptions of local initiatives. The internet resources include examples of information literacy homepages at various universities, Web-based articles and documents, and locally produced documents.

Information Literacy Skills Program Home Page
< http://www.gu.edu.au/gwis/ins/infolit/home.htm>

From Griffith University in Australia, this home page provides details about the school's information literacy program. Some of the information is designed for students, and discusses meeting requirements, etc. More interesting to nonstudents will be the lengthy "Information Literacy Blueprint," which describes plans for the development of a widespread program at Griffith University.

Internet Classrooms
< http:www.rims.k12.ca.us/SCORE/classact.html>

Provides information and links for elementary and secondary teachers on using the Internet to facilitate the development of information literacy. Includes an outline of the problem-based learning process, criteria for evaluating Internet resources, descriptions of information literacy competencies, the Big Six Skills, and Internet museum resources useful for the classroom.

Ocotillo Reports
<http://hakatai.mcli.dist.maricopa.edu/ocotillo/report.html>
These reports (1993-1996) provide details about the development of information literacy within the Maricopa County Community Colleges in Arizona.

Winhall Elementary School Library
<http://www.wcsu.k12.vt.us/~winhall/libwin.htm>
This school library site provides data and links relevant to teachers. The section under "Curriculum" includes several well-developed information literacy lesson plans, and a description of K-6 information competencies.

WWW sites were selected and annotated by Dane Ward, a librarian in the Undergraduate Library at Wayne State University.

INDEX

by Linda Webster